A Parent's Guide to Chess

Dan Heisman

2002
Russell Enterprises, Inc.
Milford, CT USA

A Parent's Guide to Chess

ISBN: 1-888690-12-7

Published by:
Russell Enterprises, Inc.
234 Depot Road
Milford, CT 06460 USA

http://www.chesscafe.com
hwr@chesscafe.com

Cover design by OutExcel! Corp., Al Lawrence, President; Kathleen Merz, Art Director.

Printed in the United States of America

Table of Contents

Acknowledgments

I would like to thank Hanon Russell, the publisher of **ChessCafe.com**, for bringing this book to market so that chess parents, and thus the world of chess, can benefit. Special kudos to Taylor Kingston, **ChessCafe.com**'s thoughtful editor, who made the text more readable and therefore more helpful.

Secondly, I would like to thank Brian Karen, who helped brainstorm the project and lay out the book's structure.

Next, I would like to thank Lois Deckelbaum and Barbara Schoener, who provided Appendix C, *Special Issues for Moms*, and Michele White, who originally suggested this very helpful feature. I would also like to thank Steve Shutt, chess coach of several times national champion Masterman High School, who suggested using the spectator guidelines presented in Appendix B.

I would also like to thank Jeff Coakley of Canada's Chess'n Math Association for providing material specific to his organization.

Finally, I would like to thank all the parents, organizers, tournament directors, and everyone else associated with the growing world of scholastic chess. Most of them perform their tasks as volunteers. Their efforts seldom receive any fanfare, but their contributions are extremely helpful, even necessary, and are appreciated more than they probably will ever know.

Dan Heisman
March 2002

Introduction

Welcome to the wonderful world of chess! The royal game offers many benefits to players of all ages. This book is intended as a guide to help parents explore this expanding world and to maximize its benefits for their children. Putting all this information in one place will, we hope, make your journey a lot easier.

The movie *Searching for Bobby Fischer* was a phenomenal success, and served as a catalyst for the growth of scholastic chess in North America. In 1990, only about 10% of tournament chess players in the US were under age 19; today, over half are! So you are one of a large group of parents who are "Searching for More Guidance" about this wonderful hobby.

The US and Canadian Chess Federations

Most organized chess is played in tournaments run by affiliates of national chess federations. Part of this book is aimed at helping a parent learn more about these federations and how you can use them to maximize your child's enjoyment and involvement.

The US Chess Federation (USCF) is a not-for-profit organization headquartered in Newburgh, New York. It serves as the official US arm of FIDE, the international chess federation. The USCF performs many of the normal functions of any organization: it coordinates its members, provides a periodic magazine, sells equipment, formulates rules, establishes affiliates, certifies directors, holds national championships, and promotes the game. It also rates the performance of its members in a very scientific manner. Scholastic players usually become keenly interested in the rating system, as it enables them accurately to measure their progress. Chapter 4 includes more information on the rating system.

The Chess Federation of Canada (CFC) is a Canadian Charitable organization headquartered in Ottawa. It is the official Canadian representative to FIDE and has functions very similar to the USCF, promoting chess for all ages.

The USCF provides a fine booklet titled *A Guide to Scholastic Chess*. Readers who are involved with school programs should request a free copy of this booklet by calling 1-800-388-KING or via www.uschess.org. This booklet is primarily aimed at administrators and teachers. Therefore this book, *A Parent's Guide to Chess*, intends to fill a scholastic void by helping parents with their individual concerns; it should also be very helpful to anyone involved with scholastic chess.

What is Scholastic Chess?

Scholastic chess is usually defined to include school-age students from grades K-12. Even pre-kindergarten children sometimes compete in scholastic events, and pre-college students below age 19 who are not affiliated with a school may also be eligible for scholastic events.

Scholastic chess encompasses a number of activities, such as school clubs, school team matches, and local, state, national, and even international tournaments and titles. There are many private clubs devoted exclusively to scholastic play, although most clubs and tournaments are "open" with regard to age; that is, they allow players of all ages to participate. It is not unusual at a chess tournament to see a 10-year-old playing someone who is 65  – and maybe the 10-year-old is the big favorite!

Besides its monthly adult magazine *Chess Life*, the USCF has a periodical devoted exclusively to its younger members: *SchoolMates*. The CFC's magazine is *En*

Passant, which is published bi-monthly. There are many chess books, web-sites, and software titles aimed primarily or exclusively at young players; these subjects are discussed in several sections of this book.

Besides the official state organizations, there are other organizations devoted to scholastic chess, for example the *Chess-in-Schools* program (formerly the *American Chess Foundation*), The *Chess Education Association*, an independent US chess program, and *Chess'n Math*, a Canadian organization which has its own magazine, *Scholar's Mate*.

The Parent's Role

Chess provides an excellent opportunity for a parent to strengthen the relationship with his or her child. While some parents are busy and cannot actively get involved, those who do often find it both rewarding and interesting. Ways in which a parent can become involved might include one or more of the following:

❖ Learn about the world of chess – This helps the parent guide his child to the maximum benefits and pleasures of playing and interacting in this arena.

❖ Learn about the game of chess – Learn to play (better) yourself. This will enable you to play with your child and understand the games they play with other children. For example, you can purchase a chess book like Grandmaster Patrick Wolff's excellent beginner's work *The Complete Idiot's Guide to Chess* or the author's *Everyone's Second Chess Book*, and read out loud or review what you have learned with your child.

❖   Provide encouragement – Chess, like any other activity rich in content, is filled with highs and lows. Parents are often rewarded by teaching their children that while winning is a positive goal, losing is not "bad" – it provides a learning opportunity, and that even the best players have lost many games but always learned from them. Parents should encourage their children to study and play their best; like many other activities, you get out what you put in – and chess is attractive in that it is ultimately fair: those who put in more effort derive more benefits.

❖   Take the student to chess activities – Visit a local club or two and attend tournaments. Tournaments vary greatly in size and type. Parents of serious chess students often travel with them to out-of-town tournaments for added interest and enjoyment.

❖   Provide local publicity and sponsorship – Local papers and media outlets usually don't know about the chess world unless someone notifies them. If you are a good writer, you can write media releases, or maybe visit or call the paper. You can also help find sponsors, who provide for better tournaments and prizes. One selling point is that chess sponsorships require less funding than most other scholastic sports!

❖   Communicate with other parents and people involved in chess. Parents can take turns carpooling students to events, and often form a network that keeps them up-to-date on the activities of the chess world and helps them to find the best tournaments, books, instructors, web-sites, and clubs for their students.

❖   Work with schools and scholastic clubs – Help your local schools and clubs support scholastic chess. Visit with your child's school to see if it has a chess program and, if so, what you can do to help. If it doesn't have one, maybe you can encourage the administrators to start one by sharing some of the information provided in this book.

Who Should Read this Book?

While the intended reader of this book is a parent of a young chess player, there is plenty of information for:

❖   Scholastic organizers and aspiring tournament directors, School teachers and administrators interested in organizing a scholastic club; and

❖   Young chess players.

Scope

There inevitably will be something you would have liked to see in *A Parent's Guide to Chess* which was omitted, or information that became out-of-date the moment it was printed. The references inside, such as chess web-sites, should provide the reader with up-to-date answers to most questions you may have. I checked all the web references before the book went to the publisher, but inevitably some of these addresses may have changed by the time you read this.

Other media material definitely complements *A Parent's Guide to Chess*. In particular, my *Everyone's 2nd Chess Book* can be considered almost a companion volume, emphasizing the playing side of the game to players of all ages and their instructors, including special sections on chess etiquette, common misconceptions, misunderstood rules, etc.

A small amount of important information has been intentionally included in two or three different places because it pertains to multiple subjects, such as *Registering for tournaments* and *Enhancing your tournament experience*. Usually the material is presented in slightly different contexts. We hope the repetition will make it easier to locate, and provide different perspectives on this worthwhile information.

Gender

While most of the chess world is male, there is a growing interest in chess among females of all ages. This book was written for all sons and daughters, so please forgive my use of "he" instead of "he/she" – my pronouns are meant to apply to all!

Opinion

It is impossible to serve the reader without occasionally offering opinions, such as which books I feel are most helpful, or which type of chess clock appears to be the most popular. The opinions are solely those of the author, and do not represent those of the publisher or anyone else. The reader is encouraged to do further research and to seek out other opinions to help form his own.

In addition, it would also be impossible to include references to all the myriad books and web-sites that may be of use to the reader. An interested parent should reference additional recommendations, like those at my web-site, or do web searches to augment my limited lists.

Contact the Author

Any comments or questions are welcome and can be directed to the author:

e-mail: danheisman@comcast.net
web: http://mywebpages.comcast.net/danheisman/chess.htm

Dan Heisman
March 2002

CHAPTER 1

Why Should My Child Play Chess?

Why should a child play chess? A short and effective answer might be:

- ❖ Chess is fun, and
- ❖ Chess is good for you.

Everyone picks a hobby that is fun, so your child likely finds chess fun or you would not be reading this book. So let's skip directly to why chess is good for you.

There are direct and indirect benefits to playing chess:

 Chess, as a mental exercise, strengthens the brain, resulting in better mental development in youngsters. For the same reason, playing chess benefits adults, especially seniors, who need active mental pastimes to help them stay alert as they get older.

Participation in chess for youngsters has many social and emotional side benefits. Several are discussed below.

Grades and Standardized Tests

The web pages www.uschess.org/scholastic/sc-research.html and amchess.org/research/ are devoted to the benefits of chess. The former lists 11 research articles and 29 supplementary articles. Many cover the direct benefits, but others concentrate more on the indirect.

Here are the findings of a study cited in one of those articles, *Chess in Education Research Summary* by Dr. Robert Ferguson, a leading expert on the benefits of chess:

During the 1995-96 school year, two classrooms were selected in each of five schools. Students (N=112) were given instruction in chess and reasoning in one classroom in each school. Pupils in the chess program scored significantly higher reading scores at the end of the year ... Why does chess have this impact?

Briefly, there appear to be at least seven significant factors:

1. Chess accommodates all modality strengths.

2. Chess provides a far greater quantity of problems for practice.

3. Chess offers immediate punishments and rewards for problem solving.

4. Chess creates a pattern or thinking system that, when used faithfully, breeds success. The chess playing students had become accustomed to looking

for more and different alternatives, which resulted in higher scores in fluency and originality.

5. Competition. Competition fosters interest, promotes mental alertness, challenges all students, and elicits the highest levels of achievement (Stephan, 1988).

6. A learning environment organized around games has a positive effect on students' attitudes toward learning. The affective dimension acts as a facilitator of cognitive achievement (Allen & Main 1976) ...

Instructive gaming is one of the most motivational tools in the good teacher's repertoire. Children love games. Chess motivates them to become willing problem solvers and spend hours quietly immersed in logical thinking. These same young people often cannot sit still for fifteen minutes in the traditional classroom.

7. Chess supplies a variety and quality of problems. As Langen (1992) states: "The problems that arise in the 70-90 positions of the average chess game are, moreover, new. Contexts are familiar, themes repeat, but game positions never do. This makes chess good grist for the problem-solving mill."

Another article that appeared in *Chess Life* magazine in 1998, "Chess and Standard Test Scores" by James M. Liptrap, began with this summary:

Regular (non-honors) Elementary students who participated in a school chess club showed twice the improvement of non-chessplayers in Reading and Mathematics between third and fifth grades on the Texas Assessment of Academic Skills…

Indirect Benefits

While more difficult to prove than academic improvement, the indirect benefits of playing chess are nonetheless real. They can help youngsters in many ways, including:

❖   Dealing with success and adversity – Whether it be wins and losses, prizes, or just public performance, chess allows students to deal with the highs and lows of competition. While most chess activities are low-key, for a small child even small events may take on significance.

❖ Teamwork – Many scholastic events have team awards, and students learn to support others on their team in a positive manner.

❖ Socialization – My son views chess tournaments as one big pizza and Chinese food party.

❖ Organization – Several studies have noted positive results in this area. Not only does a student have to organize his chess study, but also his game books, pieces, board, clock, schedule, etc. But perhaps most of all, he needs to learn to organize his thoughts to produce a logical move, and this carries over to other similar activities.

❖ Fair Play and Work Yielding Just Rewards – While nothing is perfectly fair, chess is about as good as it gets. The students who study the most and play the  most almost always tend to be better players, no matter who is more talented. Youngsters appreciate this. As a counter-example, if they took up sprinting then almost no amount of work would enable them to win a race against another youngster who is appreciably faster. However, in chess you can catch almost anyone whom you are consistently outworking.

❖ Dealing with Others – This aspect of the chess world is so important that it will have its own sub-section further on. You meet all types of players in the chess world, young and old, good players and bad. Being paired against an adult during a chess activity may provide your child his first opportunity to deal with an adult on an equal basis.

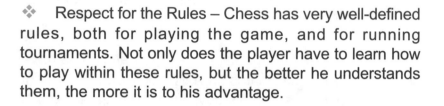

It might be a similar experience when playing much older or younger children. A youngster also has to learn how to deal with the occasional irritating opponent, and those lessons are also helpful outside the chess arena.

❖   Respect for the Rules – Chess has very well-defined rules, both for playing the game, and for running tournaments. Not only does the player have to learn how to play within these rules, but the better he understands them, the more it is to his advantage.

❖   Patience – A good chess player knows when to push his advantage and how not to try for more than his position demands. Also, youngsters tend to play too quickly, so learning to play more slowly (and consequently better) is one of the most important chess lessons he can learn.

❖   Selflessness – A chess player who thinks his moves are more important than his opponent's will soon find out that he needs to think of the other's moves as just as important. Beginners who only consider their own moves remain beginners until they can think about what both sides might be able to do. In addition, players who do not respect their opponents and behave poorly soon get a bad reputation in the chess community.

❖   Playing Quietly – You would not believe how many parents think this is their youngster's most incredible achievement. A chess playing hall is kept quiet by the tournament director, so a young player has to learn to play quietly and talk only in certain situations.

There are many other indirect benefits. For example, *leadership* might come into play if your student joins a club. *Dependability* becomes a factor when he has to learn when to be ready for the next round. *Consistency* is required: a child learns to play in the correct manner on each move or suffer the consequences. *Cooperation* with the other players and the tournament director is required. You can probably add a few more. The bottom line is clear: chess is a disciplined activity with many side benefits.

Finally, a child who plays chess is participating in an organized, fun activity in which they can share their feelings with their parents. Anyone who has seen *Searching for Bobby Fischer* knows that this was a main theme of the movie and one of its positive messages.

College and Scholarships

Chess can help you get into college and can even be the basis for a full scholarship! Recently both Princeton and the University of Chicago announced that they are giving more weight to mental sports, such as chess, in their admissions considerations, and two universities give full and partial chess scholarships (!):

❖ University of Texas, Dallas (honors) campus (www.utdallas.edu/orgs/chess/email.html)

❖ University of Maryland, Baltimore County Campus (www.umbc.edu/chess/)

At the 2001 National High School Championship, the University of Texas offered my son a full chess scholarship!

No one was more surprised (by their offer and the entire situation) than I! But this unexpected offer is great proof that chess can be much more than a secondary hobby.

Chess and American Culture

It is a profession for some, but a hobby for most. It is primarily a mental activity. Studies show it is good for you. Young participants who do well are called "prodigies."

Chess? No! Music, of course!

But if music and chess are so alike, why does American culture embrace and encourage music so much, while almost frowning at times on chess? I would like to relate a short story illustrating this imbalance.

Within the past few years I contacted my son's school district about hosting chess tournaments. After not returning my calls over a period of months, the local administration office finally told me, "We are undergoing construction at all the district's schools over the next four years and cannot host any activities." (!)

"At every school at once? All activities? Doesn't that mean all after-school clubs and football games and fund-raisers all have to be cancelled, too? For four years?"

"Well, maybe two."

This is a true story. I consider myself one of the better chess instructors in the country and, as the Scholastic Coordinator for Pennsylvania, I was not exactly without credentials. But I felt like I was being treated as if I had offered to host a symposium advocating bad manners!

If the person making the offer had been Van Cliburn or Elton John, I don't think that would have been the response. In that case, the mayor and a large crowd would have been part of the welcoming committee. The school district spends tens of thousands of dollars on band, orchestra, and choir at all levels of the district. But chess? "Don't call us; we'll call you."

In Europe the respect for chess is much greater. In Russia chess players receive strong respect and occasionally win their "Professional Athlete of the Year" award. In North America chess is often viewed as a hobby for "nerds," and that is not cool. Secondly, chess players are quiet when playing, so the activity is looked upon by some as anti-social. But most of all, *chess cannot easily be appreciated by non-players.*

Almost everyone likes listening to music of one form or the other. Music evokes emotions, and good music can be appreciated even if the person next door has a different idea of what good music is.

Not so with chess. Non-players cannot follow it, so the spectator aspect is diminished.

Finally, chess is competitive. We see that as good in physical sports, but somehow it earns a mental sport a lower rung on the cultural ladder than music. I don't see North American cultural attitudes toward chess changing very quickly. Nonetheless, as more studies prove the benefits of chess, and movies such as *Searching for Bobby Fischer* show it as a legitimate youth activity, attitudes are changing for the better. Additional support comes from the fact that more young women are playing as scholastic chess grows.

My wife put it succinctly: "I wouldn't have given chess a thought when I was younger, but now that I am familiar with the chess  scene, if I had to do it all over again, I would have played. The youngsters who play chess are, for the most part, smart, well-mannered, and good role models. It would have been a great way to meet some attractive guys!"

Chapter 2

Getting Started

2.1 When is a Child Ready to Play Chess?

There is a difference between when a child is ready to learn chess rules, and when he is ready to play in a social setting, such as a scholastic tournament. At a tournament or club the child must be able to play quietly, follow standard rules, and publicly tolerate losing.

Most children can learn how to play before age seven, and many can play reasonably before they turn six. In order  to play a complete game, they must understand not only how all the pieces move, but also the concepts of taking turns, checkmate, draws (including stalemate), promotion, and other non-move-related rules. The idea that players take turns is usually learned from simpler games, and likely will not give beginners much difficulty. On the other hand, understanding checkmate requires a little more sophistication, as the idea of "checkmating" a king involves *not* its capture, but its inability to avoid capture on the next move, and this concept often gives youngsters some difficulty.

Ready to Play in Tournaments

Many youngsters are able to move the pieces correctly, but are not yet able to sit and play quietly. While this is fine for games against a relative or friend, it is usually not tolerated in formal play. Since chess requires concentration, it is not fair to opponents or players nearby if a player is attempting conversations. The principal things a player is allowed to say (quietly) during formal competitions are restricted to comments directly allowed by the rules, such as "Do you want a draw?" or "That move is illegal" or "You touched my bishop; you have to take it."

Another prerequisite for formal play is to understand rules that do not involve moving the pieces. For example, a player must recognize when something unusual is happening at the board, and have the presence of mind to stop his game and get the tournament director, to ask a question or make a claim. Many young players try to resolve conflicts directly with their opponents and, without adequate knowledge of the rules, often arrive at unfair or illegal resolutions. It is also helpful if the student learns how to read a tournament pairing sheet, which tells him which number board he is playing on, which color pieces he has, and also learns how to mark up his result at the end of the game without continual parental or tournament director aid.

While many students are ready at six or seven to handle the mental aspects of the game, quite a few are not ready for the emotional side. Since chess does not outwardly involve luck, many students realize that losses are not easily blamed on outside factors, and thus take losing very personally. This fear of losing does not affect young students only, but they are more likely to react to losses in a manner that indicates they are not ready to play socially, such as crying, blaming the opponent, creating a physical problem such as upsetting the board, etc. We will address this issue in more detail in Section 6.3, Dealing with Highs and Lows, but how a child deals with these emotional issues is often more important than the mental ones in determining when the child is ready to play chess "with the outside world."

There is also a similar question: "What is the best age to learn and start playing in tournaments *if you are going to become a 'good' player* ?"

This is a more difficult question. Bobby Fischer was already the US Champion by age fourteen, and he started at age seven. Josh Waitzkin, of *Searching for Bobby Fischer* fame, was the US Primary (K-3) Champion and later a master at 13. On the other hand my student Danny Benjamin, who was in the same grade as Josh, did not start playing in tournaments until he was 11, but by the time Danny was 13 he and Josh were the only 13-year-old masters in the US. This late start for a young master is unusual, so the answer to the question about when champions start is "The sooner the better." Most strong players start playing in tournaments well before age eleven, and seven is probably closer to the average. But some young prodigies start at four or five and do very well!

There is not much difference in being ready to play in scholastic tournaments, and being ready to play in clubs that allow players of all ages: both require some maturity, knowing the rules, and the ability to play quietly.

However, participating in *scholastic* clubs – clubs that specialize in young players – is quite different. These clubs are often noisy and a few sniffles are easily tolerated, so players of any age are usually welcome. While no one likes a bully or a sore loser, often these clubs are a great place to find other players of about the same ability or age, and to learn the kind of discipline and chess etiquette that will enable them also to play in tournaments. Unfortunately, it is sometimes easier to find scholastic tournaments, which are held consistently all over North America, than it is to find clubs that specialize in scholastic play, unless you are lucky enough either to live in an area where one already exists or have an ongoing one at your school.

2.2 The World of Chess

Your child is ready to play someone outside your home – great! It is a big world full of clubs, tournaments, prizes, titles, and other neat stuff. Let us introduce you to that world …

FIDE and National Chess Federations

We have already familiarized you with the US and Canadian Chess Federations in the Introduction, but the real place to start is one level above them at the Fédération Internationale des Échecs (FIDE) or, in English, the International Chess Federation (www.fide.com). This is the governing body of world chess, which awards international titles (e.g. "grandmaster") and handles all international chess business. There are over 200 countries affiliated with FIDE, and each affiliate is a national chess federation.

National federations publish their *Official Rules of Chess*, which tells everyone things like:

❖ How the pieces move

❖ What is checkmate and stalemate

❖ Touch-move rules (i.e. "If you touch a piece you have to move it.")

❖ Score-keeping (writing down and recording of moves)

❖ Time controls (clocked games played under a time limit)

And much, much more, such as how a tournament director is allowed to hold and direct a chess tournament.

National federations do much more than publish the rules, of course. The following provides a sample of the USCF and CFC missions:

The USCF *(www.uschess.org)*:

❖ Sanctions chess tournaments, including 25 national championship events.

❖ Sponsors participation of Americans in international events and helps them petition for FIDE titles, such as International Grandmaster or International Arbiter.

❖ Maintains the USCF rating system.

❖ Publishes magazines. *SchoolMates* is quarterly and is designed for members 14 and under; *Chess Life* is monthly and is designed for all members older than 14.

❖ From the USCF web-site: "*As a not-for-profit membership organization, the USCF applies its revenue to services and programs benefiting its members and chess in America.*"

The CFC *(www.chess.ca)*:

❖ From the CFC web-site: "*The Chess Federation of Canada (C.F.C.) is a charitable organization (10691 2058 RR) whose mandate is to promote and encourage the knowledge, study and play of the game of chess in Canada. The C.F.C. organizes National Championships (Canadian Closed, Canadian Women's Closed, Canadian Junior and Canadian Youth Chess Championship), and provides funding for the winners to go on to the World Championships. In addition, the C.F.C. has sent a team to the World Chess Olympiad each time it has been held (every second year) since 1964."*

Independent Organizations

As mentioned in the Introduction, there are many non-federation organizations devoted to scholastic chess. Three of the largest are the *Chess-in-Schools* Program, the *Chess Education Association*, and the Canadian *Chess'n Math*. Membership in these organizations is sometimes free, in which case their costs are borne by the tournament or per-game entry fees.

Chess in the Schools (www.chessintheschools.org), was formerly known as the American Chess Foundation. Their web-site states their mission: "Chess-in-the-Schools (CIS) is a non-profit organization that teaches chess to New York City public school children as a means of enhancing critical  thinking skills, self-esteem, discipline, and socialization. Working in close partnership with Title 1 elementary and junior high schools, we provide instruction, equipment, and the support necessary to achieve demonstrable student success." I would add that CIS teaches in more than just New York. I worked for them for three years as an instructor in the Philadelphia Public School System.

The *Chess Education Association* (www.chesslogic.com) is a parallel organization to the USCF, which offers their *Scholastic Chess Webzine* to its members and has separate tournaments and ratings. Their mission: "1) More chess in more schools for more children, and 2) A dedication to teach children positive life values through the chess experience."

The Canadian *Chess'n Math Association* (www.chess-math.org) is Canada's national scholastic chess organization. It was established in 1985 as a non-profit organization and is dedicated to promoting youth chess in Canada. They currently have offices in Toronto, Montreal, and Hull, with 15 full-time employees and 60 qualified chess instructors. Chess'n Math runs monthly scholastic  tournaments, conducts regular chess classes and camps, provides instructors for school chess programs, and operates chess shops in Canada's two largest cities. Numerous affiliates across Canada run local Chess'n Math tournaments. It has its own scholastic magazine, *Scholar's Mate*, which is published 5 times per year.

Overview of Clubs and Tournaments

National federations also certify Tournament Directors (TDs) to run *tournaments*, and they affiliate and help organized chess *clubs* throughout their countries.

The following illustrates the difference between a chess club and a chess tournament. More information about clubs can be found in Section 2.6, Where Does One Play?, and about tournaments in Chapter 5, Tournament Participation.

A club is group of people, usually incorporated as not-for-profit, who meet periodically to play chess. The meeting period is often weekly, but some large metropolitan clubs are open daily. One can walk into a chess club and find people ready and willing to play chess. Some chess clubs are just for young players, but most allow members of any age ("open"). Some clubs play "rated," formal games, while others have little or no organized activities other than providing a place for its members to play – it is up to each club to decide how it wants to organize its activities. Clubs usually charge a nominal fee for annual dues to cover the costs of the meeting room, correspondence, snacks, etc.

On the other hand, a tournament is a one-time event, usually with an entry fee and prizes. When a player is ready to play in rated tournaments, he will join his national federation, as is usually required to play in a rated event and receive a rating. US tournaments and their associated information are listed at www.uschess.org/tla and in the back of *Chess Life* and *School Mates* magazines.

The tournament information in US magazines is called the Tournament Life Announcements (TLAs). TLAs allow members to find out where the tournaments are, when they are held, entry fees, prizes, eligibility, contact information, etc. Almost all listed tournaments are "rated" by the USCF, which is to say that after the tournament the TD will send in a "Rating Report" to the USCF and all participants will receive new or updated ratings." In addition, the USCF requires that all participants of rated tournaments must be members of the USCF (you can always join your national federation during registration at the tournament if you are not a member),

Once the tournament has been rated by the federation, all formerly unrated participants will be given a rating. The ratings of players who already are rated will be affected by the outcome of their games. When they win their rating goes up and when they lose their rating goes down. The higher the player you beat, the more your rating goes up, etc. More on ratings in Section 4.2.5, Ratings and Prizes. The CFC ratings operate in a similar manner.

Most tournaments are "open" – you do not have to live in a particular place, or be of any specific age, to play. You just walk in, pay the entry fee, and play. Others are restricted in some way – the most usual restriction is a scholastic tournament, which is only open to those in grades 12 and below.

Most scholastic tournaments are run by the "Swiss" system. That means that no one is eliminated and in each round a player is paired with someone who is doing as well as he is. So if your child is playing in his first tournament and loses his first three games, he will be paired in the fourth round against another weak player who has also lost his first three games. In this way each participant gets to "find his level" as the tournament progresses. So in the long run, players generally find most games competitive and fun under the Swiss system.

2.3 Typical Progression Through Chess

Now that you know some of the major pieces of the chess world, here is a typical youngster's progression through chess:

First he will learn how to play chess from a parent, friend, beginner's book, or even a couple of lessons from a local chess instructor. A parent should make sure he gets all the common rules correct, especially promotion (multiple queens allowed), castling (the king moves 2 squares no matter which side you castle), *en passant*, the different kinds of draws (3-fold repetition of position, 50-move rule, stalemate, lack of mating material, etc.). These are best learned from an experienced player, a good book, or a lesson. It is not a good idea to start playing with the wrong rules!

Next he should play at least few dozen games in a fairly short period of time to get to recognize the pieces, how they move, and the basic rules. This can be done with a relative, neighbor, computer, or friend. Much of the information that is picked up during this time, such as "board vision" and basic playing guidelines, is covered in *Everyone's 2nd Chess Book*.

If your child really likes the game and wants to continue to improve, he might:

❖ Learn how to keep score in algebraic notation (covered in most beginners books and at my web-site);

❖ Purchase a decent set, clock, and scorebook (see Section 2.7);

❖ Join the national federation and start playing in scholastic chess tournaments;

❖ Join a chess club to play periodically against better competition; and/or

❖ Play on the Internet with servers like the Internet Chess Club (ICC at www.chessclub.com). For more information, see Chapter 3.

As a child progresses, he will continue to play in clubs and tournaments, with the computer, and with friends. If you see that your child is serious and wants to work to get better, then by all means consider taking lessons from a professional chess instructor. Lessons will help identify both things your child is doing that can be improved, and a method for doing so efficiently, so improvement will be greatly facilitated. All really good players have had steady coaches when they were learning, just as a good musician learns from someone who plays the same instrument.

Do Kids Play Without a Break?

Parents sometimes ask me: "My child is losing interest in chess and wants to stop playing right now – do you think this is normal?" Answer: yes. Many children start in chess, stop for a while, decide they miss it, then start again. In fact, in my experience it's relatively rare for child, especially a younger one, to stick with chess as a hobby continuously into his college years, adulthood, or throughout life. Generally the younger a child starts, the more likely he is to have one or more periods when he loses interest in chess. The table below shows some educated estimates of the trend, based on my experience. On the left is the age at which the child starts chess, on the right the percentage of that group that take a break from chess, at least temporarily, at some point before they reach college age:

6: 90%
7: 85%
8: 75%
9: 67%
10: 60%
11: 50%
12: 40%
13: 25%
14+: 20%

In other words, only one child in ten who starts playing chess at age 6 will maintain his interest continuously through age 18. But this does not mean these youngsters quit chess permanently. It appears that common scenarios are for a child to stop around age 7-9 and start again at 10-12, or to stop around age 9-12 and start again as a adult. So if your child drops chess for a while, do not be concerned. He'll come back to it when he's ready.

2.4 In Loco parentis Issues

It is important for parents to understand which chess activities are *in loco parentis* (in lieu of a parent – that is, situations where someone will watch your children for you) and which are not. However, nothing written in this section is guaranteed – if your child is at an age where this is important to you, then you MUST check with the organizer or director of each activity to make sure and, when in doubt, do NOT drop off a young child without supervision.

Here are sample events and a guide to whether they might normally serve *in loco parentis*:

❖ After-school activity: <u>usually</u> (that is, usually will be *in loco parentis* – will not require parental supervision)

❖ Scholastic chess club: <u>maybe</u>

❖ Adult chess club: <u>usually not</u>

❖ Scholastic chess tournament: <u>usually not</u>

❖ Open chess tournament: <u>almost always not</u>

How to handle this issue varies widely with the age and responsibility of the child, and the locale of the chess event. For example, a child of 10 who can be dropped off at the local chess club for a couple of hours cannot as easily be left alone at a big-city open tournament. An immature 12-year-old might be more likely to get into trouble than a mature 10-year-old. So it is worth repeating: *When in doubt, do not leave a child without supervision and never assume that just because the tournament is "organized" and invites scholastic players that someone will automatically be responsible for watching your child!*

2.5 The Role of a National Federation in Scholastic Chess

All national federations promote scholastic chess. Section 4.6 addresses National Championships, but a federation's involvement is much deeper than just running tournaments. The USCF and CFC do all the things for their scholastic members that they do for adult members, such as promote chess, provide ratings, publish a magazine, sell equipment, etc. However, a federation has an increased focus on its future members, as it should, for two reasons:

1) The health of any organization is fortified by promoting its future, and

2) The percentage of scholastic tournament players has grown enormously in the past few years, again partly due to the movie *Searching for Bobby Fischer.* For example, in the USCF:

❖   In 1991 there were fewer than 10,000 members age 18 or below from a total of about 55,000 (about 18%)

❖   By 2001 over 47,000 of the 90,000 members were below age 18 (about 52%!). An ongoing graph of USCF membership is provided at detroitchess.com/memgraph.htm.

If any other large organization had gone from 18% to 52% youth membership, I am sure that would attract growing attention, too! How has this growth been met?

❖   The USCF has established both a Director of Scholastic Programs and a National Scholastic Advisory Council.

❖   The USCF now directly oversees its large national scholastic championships, which are the biggest chess tournaments in the US every year. 4,700 played at the

SuperNationals in Kansas City in 2001. The CFC runs the Canadian Youth Chess Championships; these national events are discussed in Section 4.6, Important Scholastic Tournament and Titles.

❖   More emphasis is being placed on chess training, both in manpower and materials.

❖   Special rules for scholastic tournaments are now being created and considered, since many young players have special concerns (e.g. inability to keep score) that are unusual in adults. For example, intimidation and cheating are easier because in beginners' scholastic tournaments the spectators are more likely to be larger and more knowledgeable than the players, so rules to ensure fairness are even more important than with adults.

2.6 Where Does One Play?

The first place young players play is at home with parents and friends. This is a great way to start because the surroundings are familiar, it is easy to get there, and the competition is friendly. However, there are potential drawbacks:

❖   Dad or Mom may be a better player than Junior (or Dad/Mom doesn't want to play Junior), so Dad sometimes thinks he should throw games to keep Junior happy (this is not usually a good idea unless the child is very small and takes losing far too seriously).

❖   It gets boring playing the same opponents game after game.

❖   The neighbor's son or daughter may play much less often, so when your son becomes fascinated with chess, he quickly improves, and playing the neighbor results in a large percentage of wins and possibly some hard feelings.

❖ A young player can get into bad habits by playing only weaker players. For example, in *Everyone's 2nd Chess Book* I discuss how players learn to make bad threats because their weak opponents often don't see them, and when these succeed they come to believe that making bad threats is a good idea, and thus develop the bad habit of doing so regularly.

❖ Games at home are often played without a clock. In the long run this is less fun, and in the short run playing without a clock can lead to bad time-management habits. Usually playing with clocks helps a child slow down his play and think more correctly. Ironically, when a child first plays with a clock he may think it is now a "time race" and play even faster, with disastrous results. A little experience with clock play will go a long way toward developing better time-management habits.

❖ Everyone might be playing by the wrong rules. For example, many young players don't know *en passant* or erroneously believe that when promoting a pawn they can only get back a piece that was captured.

Eventually most parents search for outside for places to play. Usually a phone book does not list "Chess Clubs," so what can you do?

❖ Look in the local paper under "Calendar" or "Activities."

❖ Check with a library or your child's school.

❖ Look in a book like *A Parent's Guide to Chess*!

❖   Ask neighbors if they know of any places that have periodic, organized chess.

❖   Search for chess places on the World Wide Web.

I often get phone calls from local people who searched on the web and found my national federation, which in turn recommended the state affiliate, which then referred them to me.

Clubs

It is only natural for a parent to seek out a chess club for the child to join and play. The main problem is that outside of schools, there are relatively few clubs that are exclusively for young players, so the closest one may not be nearby. The availability of nearby "scholastic-only" clubs varies greatly from community to community.

Here in Pennsylvania, Pittsburgh has some large youth clubs, while Philadelphia scholastic chess is more school-oriented. Therefore, your child may not be able to find a scholastic-only club close enough for your driving comfort, and you may have to settle for a club open to all ages, but, which may or may not encourage young players to attend.

Clubs that are primarily for adults are not only not *in loco parentis* (young children have to be supervised), but also  do not tolerate noise or distracting behavior nearly as well as some scholastic clubs. So in many cases when a parent asks me if their child is "good enough" for clubs or tournaments, the question is really about maturity and the ability to play quietly, not necessarily about how well their child plays chess. At our local Main Line

Chess Club anyone who can play quietly and remain quiet when his game is finished, is more than welcome no matter what his age.

The USCF lists their affiliated clubs at www.uschess.org/directories/. The CFC lists theirs at www.chess.ca/chess_clubs.htm.

While many American chess clubs – and most of the best ones – are affiliated with the USCF, there are certainly others not listed. These can, for the most part, be found by the methods described in the previous section.

What else does a parent need to know about a chess club? Some of the most important points are:

❖   Dues are usually assessed on an annual basis.

❖   Activities vary greatly from club to club – some clubs feature slow, rated games, while others prefer informal, quicker games. Since federation membership is usually required to get a rating, clubs that feature rated games usually require members to join the national federation as well as the club if they are to participate in these activities.

❖   Most clubs do not offer formal instruction, but can direct you to someone who can. Others, especially some scholastic clubs, are strongly built around instruction.

❖   Some clubs supply sets and clocks; others do not. Bringing a pencil for keeping score – and your own scorebook, if you have one, is a good idea. Most clubs will supply scoresheets for their members who know how to keep score (it is a rule in tournament play that those who know how to keep score must do so).

❖   Many clubs will pair their players for the evening as the players would be paired for a tournament. Others have "open" play, where you find yourself an opponent each week.

Some clubs have formal activities which start near the beginning of each club's meeting. Members and guests who come later are welcome to play, but may have trouble joining the activity once it is in progress. Some activities are much easier to join in progress than others. Our club plays rated Swiss tournaments each month, which means that if a club member does not show up on a particular night, that causes no problems – we expect only some of our members to be there, and so design events for which constant attendance is not required.

Tournaments

Other than informal after-school get-togethers, chess tournaments are the primary places where youngsters participate in scholastic chess. In accordance with this lofty status, I have devoted the entire Chapter 4, Tournament Participation, to this subject.

Team Tournaments, Leagues, and Matches

Sometimes chess can be played as a team game. By that I don't mean that more than one person plays a side, but that multiple games count toward one goal, like winning a "match." This type of team chess can be done in several ways:

❖   Team Tournaments – tournaments where each school (or whatever constitutes a team) sends a certain number of players, and designates a Board 1, Board 2, etc., and each team is paired against another team, its Board 1 against the other team's Board 1, and so on. The team that wins the most games wins the match. There are several matches in a team tournament. Teams are paired against each other by match score in a Swiss system similar to individual tournaments (See Section 4.2).

❖ Individual Match – A school challenges another school. There are a certain number of boards and they play against each other as in a team tournament, but there are only two schools involved and usually one or two games between each board.

❖ League – Several schools form a league and periodically, for example each week, a school plays a match against one of the other schools. The school that does best in these matches wins the league title. Scoring is usually by matches won and lost, not the total of the individual games. For example, if a team wins 8 of their 10 matches of four boards each and 27 of the 40 games in those matches, they finish ahead of another school that won 7 of their 10 matches but won 28 of their 40 games.

Camps

Chess camps are held periodically, often annually in the summer. The better camps feature instruction from several well-known masters (up to Grandmaster), and usually  include some athletic opportunities like swimming or tennis. These camps can last from a few days up to a couple of weeks. At larger camps the campers are put into groups according to age and ability, and they get a concentrated dose of chess for the duration. Camps are usually advertised in federation and state/ province magazines. Among the better known camps here in the Eastern US are:

❖ Castle Chess Camp (www.amchess.org/camp/index.html) The oldest chess camp of them all – located in Bradford, PA.

❖   Kopec's Chess Camp (www.kopecchess.com) - New York and Lawrenceville, NJ. In 2001 they also had a segment at the World Open in Philadelphia.

2.7 Equipment
Standard equipment for a chess tournament includes the following:

❖   Pieces (All the pieces together can be considered a "set"; sometimes "set" can also refer to the pieces plus a board.)

❖   Board

❖   Clock

❖   Scorebook or scoresheet

❖   Writing instrument (sharpened pencil preferred)

❖   Carrying case (optional)

With the exception of some national events, most tournaments do NOT supply sets and almost none supply clocks, but most do make scoresheets available. So it is a good idea to purchase this equipment if your child is going to play in tournaments with any regularity. Equipment can be purchased from your national chess federation or any chess store. There are many chess stores, and most have web pages. The following are a sample: ChessCafe.com, Chess Digest, ChessCo, American Chess Equipment and Chess Central.

Since a chess game is played by two people, not everyone needs to have a set and clock. However, you would be surprised how many scholastic games are played between two players neither of whom brought sets, and especially between those who both lack clocks.

Therefore, it is a good idea to purchase all of the above equipment and bring it to every tournament. If you purchase an analog (non-digital) clock and use an inexpensive carrying case, the total cost can be less than $100.

While there is no standard requiring a particular set of pieces, there is a standard for set design, and this is called "Staunton." This is the design you see in most sets throughout the world, with a cross on top of the king, a crown on the queen, rooks that look like castle turrets, knights that look like horse heads, etc.

The most popular set for scholastic tournament play is a "single-weighted" plastic set with a 3¾-inch king and rollup board, available from almost any chess store.

 In general, the heavier (more "weighted") the pieces, the more stable and desirable, and the more expensive. There are double- and triple-weighted plastic sets, but they cost considerably more than a single-weighted set. The unweighted sets you can buy for a few dollars at your local toy store are not recommended: they usually cost almost as much as a single-weighted set (since toy stores do not buy chess sets in the volume a chess seller does), and they are smaller and very easy to knock over, and thus much harder to play with. Some players choose to play with the older, more expensive, wood sets. As a guideline, a set with a king smaller than 2¾" is much too small.

Along with the better plastic sets, players usually purchase inexpensive roll-up boards that are easy to carry. The most common colors are buff and green, or buff and brown. Bright colors such as red are hard on the eyes, and red and black boards are considered checkerboards. Boards should be coordinated with the size of the pieces; a piece should take up most, but not all of a square. The standard

3¼" king sets usually have boards that have 2-2¼" squares, and 2" is probably a little too small. That is why most sellers recommend a particular board or group of boards for each set. Also, it would not make sense to match an inexpensive set with an expensive board or vice versa.

Clocks are mainly analog (a traditional clock with two faces and hands) or digital. Today digital clocks are about twice as expensive as analog (roughly $100 vs. $50), but I expect digital clocks gradually to become less expensive. Most analog clocks need to be wound, and need to be checked before each game; digital clocks usually run on batteries. A good analog clock is the Rolland™ clock, and the BHB™ clocks are also popular.  Currently the most popular digital clock is a Chronos™ clock, which has large, easy-to-read features, but retails a little higher than other digital clocks.

Using the Clock
A chess clock has two faces (or on a digital clock, two time displays counting down). Each face shows the thinking time of that player. While a player is thinking, his clock is running. When a player moves, he then presses the button on his side of the clock, thus stopping his time from running and starting his opponent's time.

A player runs out of time when: (1) With an analog clock, the "flag" on his side of the clock falls after the minute hand passes 12:00, or, (2) with a digital clock, his side counts down to zero time.

If a player runs out of time and his opponent then "calls" it, the player loses (a "time forfeit") if his opponent has mating material, and draws if the opponent does not. Only a participant in the game (or under certain circumstances a

TD) can claim that time has run out. A player may have to make a given number of moves or possibly all his moves within the prescribed time period. In scholastic chess making all the moves is usually required; this is called a "sudden death" time control.

On most analog clocks, a mechanical flag is raised by the minute hand as the top of the hour approaches, and then falls when the hour is reached. On analog clocks the rule is that the first time control always ends at 6:00, so when a player's flag falls at 6:00, he has used all his time and if his opponent calls attention to this, then the player who has used all his time loses just as if he had been checkmated.

Other Equipment: Writing Utensils, Scorebooks, and Carrying Cases

I suggest bringing at least two sharpened pencils to each game. Since I advise writing down a move before it is played so that the planned move can be erased if a further "sanity check" shows it to be faulty, using a pen can get a little messy!

Scorebooks are bound scoresheets; they are inexpensive and allow for easy safekeeping of game scores. Game scores are important because:

❖   If you know how to keep score, rules require you to do so, to aid in case either player makes a claim (such as time forfeit, illegal move, threefold repetition of position draw, etc.)

❖   They provide historical documents for publishing games in bulletins, magazines, books etc. Many of the chess books your child purchases would not be possible unless someone had recorded the games!

❖   They allow for later analysis. As a chess instructor, the main focus of many of my lessons are my students' games, so having their scorebooks available is a prerequisite for a session.

I prefer scorebooks that have additional columns for recording how much time is left after each move, since I find this extra information very helpful, but any commercial scorebook is adequate.

Carrying cases vary greatly in price and style. Some only hold the pieces (a "bag"), while others have special compartments not only for pieces, set, clock, board, and scorebook, but also for additional books. So before you purchase a carrying case, compare a few to see which one best meets your child's needs.

Once you have purchased these few items, your child will be as prepared as any chess veteran!

Chapter 3

Chess and Computers

 It is impossible to discuss the world of chess without mentioning computers. Computers and chess is such a big subject that several books have been devoted exclusively to different aspects of their relationship. The subjects presented below are limited to items of interest to new chess parents. As always, I have supplied additional references for further exploration.

3.1 The World-Wide Web

Playing

There are many chess "servers" on the web, where anyone can play against all levels of players from all around the world. Some of these servers are free and others require an annual fee. The best ones require you to download special interface programs to  allow easy participation, while others (usually the ones for the masses) do not.

The best known chess server in the chess community is the Internet Chess Club (ICC; www.chessclub.com), a fee-based and professionally run service. You can also play for free on the ICC as a guest, with reduced side benefits. Other popular servers include the USCF's own server (US Chess Live!), and those at ChessNet, Yahoo, Microsoft Network, etc.

Learning About Chess

There are many sites, large and small, that provide chess information and instruction. Many of these, like my web-site (mywebpages.comcast.net/danheisman/chess.htm) and the excellent on-line chess magazine ChessCafe.com (www.chesscafe.com) are free, while others charge a membership or lesson fee. These sites range in quality from minimal to really substantial. Besides using general web search engines or using my web-site's *Link* sub-page, an excellent way to find all types of chess sites is via large, generic chess link sites such as:

- ❖ *About Chess* (chess.about.com/games/chess)
- ❖ *Chessopolis* (www.chessopolis.com)
- ❖ *The Chess Report* (members.aol.com/dals ault/index2.htm)

I produce a monthly instructional web column, *Novice Nook*, for ChessCafe.com. *Novice Nook* is aimed at adult beginners, but is equally suitable for younger students. While primarily aimed at adults, The Chess Café contains a large variety of columns and features which are helpful to players of almost all ages and levels.

Besides instruction, there are many other types of chess information available on the web. Examples of these include:

- ❖ Chess news, e.g., *The Week in Chess* (www.chesscenter.com/twic/twic.html)

- ❖ Software to help run chess tournaments, e.g. *Swis-Sys* (www.initco.net/~suits/)

- ❖ Fascinating Chess Information, e.g. *Chess Curiosities* (www.xs4all.nl/~timkr//chess/chess.html)

- ❖ Archives of chess databases, e.g. *Pittsburgh Chess Archives* (www.pitt.edu/~schach/Archives/index2.html)

For parents more interested in this large subject area, there is a recent book devoted entirely to it: *Chess on the Net*, by Mark Crowther.

The USCF website (www.uschess.org) is a very large site with a tremendous amount of chess information. Navigating this site can sometimes be difficult (for example, state organizations are currently listed under "Clubs"), but even browsing around can be exceptionally educational. At the top of many pages are links to the main sub-pages ("Tournaments", "Contact Us", etc.), while the left side usually has sub-links of the browsed page.

Some of the principal pages I use are:

❖ Ratings – Current ratings of individuals are posted at www.64.com/uscf/ratings/

❖ Upcoming tournaments – www.uschess.org/tla

❖ Club Listings – www.uschess.org/directories/clubs.html

❖ State Affiliates – www.uschess.org/directories/states.html

❖ State Scholastic Coordinators – www.uschess.org/directories/coordinators.html

❖ Instructional information for scholastic players – www.uschess.org/scholastic/

❖ News – www.uschess.org/clife/current/

The CFC website is located at www.chess.ca/. It is available in both French and English and has many sub-pages similar to the USCF website, but of course with different specific information.

3.2 Computer Software

Chess-Playing Programs

This section discusses a few of the major playing programs for the PC. The most popular commercial program, Mindscape's *ChessMaster*™ (Version 8000 is the latest), also has a Macintosh version, as do some of the other products listed below.

Overview of the Most Popular Programs

For the past few years there have been many good chess-playing programs on the market. The latest versions of these programs cost about $50, and previous versions are usually available for much less. These previous versions may be just as helpful for your child, so they are usually excellent bargains. Many of these have chess "engines" (the part that calculates the moves) based upon non-commercial programs that have competed for the World Microprocessor Championships. Set on their strongest level, these high-rated programs, including *ChessMaster* (*CM*) and *Extreme Chess*™, can play close to Grandmaster strength on modern PCs.

It is also interesting to note that while *CM* can play much better than a "fun" program like Interplay's *Battlechess*™ (*BC*), it has many settings that *BC* does not have which also allow it play much worse than even the lowest *BC* setting. Therefore, many of the best programs can be "fine-tuned" to play at almost any level, from beginner to master.

Recently, a few companies have been packaging multiple chess CDs in one package. These might include one or two of the older versions of chess-playing programs along with a few chess teaching programs (as described in section 3.2.2). These packages are usually a bargain, as the older versions are usually just as good for almost all students anyway, so you get much more for your money.

Most professional players use a program such as *Fritz 7*™ (available at www.chessbaseusa.com). While *Fritz*'s engine might be only marginally better than *CM*, it does have compatibility with chess-oriented database programs, notably *ChessBase*™, and also has some nice features specifically designed for strong players. These professional programs formerly cost about $150, but in the past few years they also have come down to about $50.

Using the Programs for Maximum Benefit

Learn how to change the settings on the computer to play different strengths. Be aware that setting an inexpensive computer (such as the older table-top ones available from *Radio Shack*) on a lower "level" usually means it just plays faster – but it is still playing the best it can, just not thinking as long. A very good program like *CM*, even its very fastest mode, will beat a beginning student virtually 100% of the time on its default setting.

Here are various ways to make *CM* play worse:

❖ Set its level to Newcomer or Novice (Under Menu, "Play", the first item)

❖ Set it to a weak "personality"such as Novice or Woodpusher (under Menu "Play" item "Set up game details" – the names scroll over the picture of the board on the right)

46

❖   Change its thinking depth to one or two ply (half-moves) or only a few seconds (Menu "Play" "Set up Game Details" use "Different Time Controls" and set them to a low value)

❖   Don't let the computer think on your move (Under "Play" item "Set up a Personality" click off "Deep Thinking")

❖   Alter the value of its parameters (Under "Play" item "Set up a Personality" change parameters). For example, you can make *CM* think a queen is worth less than a pawn!

I suggest setting a chess computer's "level" so that it will win about 75% of the games against whomever it is playing (about 200 USCF points above its opponent). This is close to optimum: if set any stronger the games will not be close and your child will learn less; any weaker and the computer will not be taking advantage of your child's mistakes, and will not push him to play above his average playing strength.

Be aware that computers "don't play like humans." Therefore, don't play exclusively with the computer. Playing humans helps one learn not only how to deal with human-type mistakes, but also how to deal with human-type behavior. The computer does not care how your child acts, but playing against a human encourages him to practice good chess etiquette, with the resulting social benefits.

Computer chess programs, while playing objectively "worse" on fast speeds, do comparatively a lot better against humans *if the human is forced to play at those same speeds*. This is because a computer can calculate millions of possibilities in a second and can play a reasonable move in a time period that to a human seems instant; even the best speed-chess-playing humans do not have this capacity, and thus humans gain comparatively more playing strength than a computer when given more time. So while the best software programs play about Grandmaster strength in slow (two-hour) play, they are definitely World Championship caliber when set to play a game in five minutes – provided the human they are playing has to play the entire game in five minutes, also.

Instructional Software

Although today most instruction is done through books and interactive web-sites, there is still a market for individually packaged chess instruction software for all ages. Some parents swear by these products. Among the commercially available ones that readily come to mind are:

❖ *Chess Mentor 2.0™*
❖ *Maurice Ashley Teaches Chess™*
❖ Convekta Products:

> *CHESS SCHOOL FOR BEGINNERS™*
> *ADVANCED CHESS SCHOOL™*
> *CHESS TACTICS FOR BEGINNERS™*

Chess Mentor (www.chess.com/) is one of the oldest programs. To quote their website:

> *Using our patented Learning Engine® environment, Chess Mentor presents you with challenges crafted by internationally respected chess teachers. You actively participate with the Learning Engine to solve these challenges with as much — or as little — help as you want. The Learning Engine continuously monitors your efforts, giving you immediate feedback, automatically providing you with review of material you have not yet mastered, and presenting you with new material only when you are ready. You learn with confidence and at your own pace.*

I have used *Chess Mentor* and can verify that it is designed for players of many different levels. You can start at any level, and the program will automatically go back to problems that you missed or did too slowly (problems are timed to get that extra dimension of learning). Their e-mail and phone support for problems, technical and otherwise, also seems fairly solid.

Maurice Ashley Teaches Chess has been a popular CD-ROM available at stores for many years, but apparently is now no longer being published. However, it is sometimes packaged with other inexpensive chess CDs and in this form is a real bargain. This CD does have some playing capabilities, but the emphasis is on fun-oriented instruction. *Maurice Ashley Teaches Chess* is probably not recommended for a teenager, since the instruction seems to be aimed at a slightly younger audience.

The three Convekta products listed above are aimed at younger audiences and are described at their website, www.chessassistant.com. In addition to these fine learning tools, Convekta (www.chessassistant.com) also has a much more advanced program, *Chess Assistant Chess Tactics Art 3.0*, which is highly recommended by several of my students.

Many, if not most, of the commercially available software playing programs discussed above also include instructional software. While not strictly instructional programs, *ChessBase™* and *Bookup™* are database-oriented products that are used by many strong players, so if your child ever becomes really proficient, he should be aware of these more advanced support tools.

Finally, a program suite that does not fit neatly into any of the above categories: The Think Like A King® School

Chess Software System has become USCF's Official Scholastic Software. Designed as a comprehensive solution for school chess programs, the software is aimed at a parent, coach, or teacher who is running a chess club or class, and includes management, motivation, and teaching functions. The foundation program, Chess Club Manager© (CCM) contains dozens of time saving and creative tools. For example, CCM lets you maintain up-to-the-minute club ratings. It is designed to be easy enough for students to use (and do most of the actual work!). Other features include the ability to award bonus points, or to print any of the following: award certificates, club management forms, and chess puzzle handouts. The puzzles come from the Chess Workouts© Series, the teaching arm of the Think Like A King® System. Further information is available at www.schoolchess.com.

The computer is one of the best tools a chess player can imagine. Learning to use it to enhance both your student's playing ability and his enjoyment is both beneficial and, in some instances, educational!

Chapter 4

Tournament Participation

4.1 Finding Out About Tournaments

Finding about tournaments is easy. Basically, there are two ways to make contact:

❖ Passive: The tournament organizer contacts you through an e-mail or a mailing, or

❖ Active: You find a tournament by looking in a magazine or web-site.

A tournament organizer can contact you only if he has your e-mail or home mailing address in his database, or If you have contacted him to let you know about future events. There are many ways of finding out about local tournament organizers, but the easiest way is by attending a tournament you discovered via method #2 and asking the Tournament Director (TD) if there is a mailing list. In the US, state scholastic coordinators are listed at www.uschess.org/directories/coordinators.html.

Once you join an organization such as the USCF, you will receive information from them about their events. As discussed earlier, the USCF sends the monthly *Chess Life* Magazine to its older members and the quarterly *School Mates* to its younger scholastic members. Each magazine has a section called "Tournament Life Announcements", or "TLAs." These sections contain listings of tournaments. Different levels of tournaments might include:

❖ Nationals – National championship events, such as the scholastic tournaments discussed in Section 4.6, or adult events, such as the US or Canadian Open.

❖ Grand Prix – Large open US events which offer fairly high cash prizes.

❖ State/Province – Local events, listed by each state or province. States are presented alphabetically.

❖ CFC-ICC – The CFC (Chess Federation of Canada) has teamed with the ICC to have joint events on the Internet.

There is sometimes a separate section at the end for "unrated" tournaments – ones that don't count toward a player's rating (advertising these nationally is relatively rare).

US TLAs are also listed on-line at www.uschess.org/tla and Canadian ones at www.chess.ca/tournaments.htm.

Once you find a TLA, it will tell you the pertinent information you need to decide to attend. The TLA section uses abbreviations to save space, but there is a legend on the first page to help newcomers decipher the text, e.g. "EF" is "Entry Fee" and "HR" is "Hotel Rates."

The TLA will say where the tournament is, how much is the entry fee, whether it is restricted to certain ages or grades, times of the rounds, the time limit for each game, etc. Finally, there is "further contact" information. This may be an address, phone number, web-site, and/or e-mail address. These are usually excellent places to contact if you want to get on a local mailing list, or find out about local clubs and tournaments.

4.2 A Typical Tournament

This section describes a typical rated chess tournament. First we will present a fictional, humorous walk-through of a student's first tournament day. The remainder of this section describes supplemental information, including Swiss system pairings, byes, ratings, etc.

4.2.1 A Day in the Life (Tournament Version)
Time to get up! Today is little Hoobley's first tournament!

Last night you double-checked the web at www.uschess.org/tla or www.chess.ca/tournaments.htm to find the time for registration. The tournament is being played at a local hotel, and Hoobley needs to join his national federation, so you want to leave a little early. Hoobley's friend, Doobley, was initially not going to go because her parents thought that she needed to be a member already to play, but you assured them that anyone could join the federation during registration. Maybe Doobley, who seemed like a pretty good player, would have a chance at an unrated prize. You had been told that experienced kids have a chess "rating" while those in their first tournament enter as "unrateds" and get a rating after the tournament results are sent to the national federation.

Upon arrival at the tournament, you see a line for registration. The good-looking TD is helping people sign up. When you get to the front of the line, he gives a federation membership form to Hoobley, who chooses to get a scholastic membership. The TD explains to you that this is a once-a-year cost and that Hoobley will get a nice magazine as part of his membership privileges. He also tells you to hold on to your receipt, which will act as your proof of membership until Hoobley's membership card arrives in the mail in a few weeks. So if Hoobley wants to play in next week's Midnight Madness tournament, that receipt will prove to the TD that he is a member. You ask the TD what you should do until the first round starts, and he says that Hoobley can play some fun, warm-up games in the skittles room until the TD can post the first-round pairings.

In the skittles room you find Doobley, who is playing blind-fold against the local chess master. She is giggling as the master tries to find a way out of her lethal trap. You notice they are playing with a chess clock.

Hoobley does not own a clock, but he has brought his new board and set (they told him not to get the one with red squares). Hoobley is now worried – will he have to play with a clock? Yes, the friendly chess master says, it is a tournament rule that you have to play with a clock, but if you don't have one, your opponent probably will. You can also start your game without a clock and, if your game starts to run too long, the TD will assign a clock to you. The chess master also tells Hoobley to relax, as he will have plenty of time to play his game, and young players often play too fast in their first tournament.

After Doobley announces mate in 17, the TD says that the first-round pairings are up. There are 2 sections, one primarily for adults, and the other for scholastic. The chess master is playing in the adult section, and is glad not to be in the same section with Doobley, who is playing in the scholastic section.

You find Hoobley's name on the pairing chart. It has his name on the right and the line says:

17 C. Brown (13)   H. Baskerville (33)

What does this mean? Someone explains that this means that Hoobley is Black on board 17 against little Charlie, and that Hoobley has pairing number 33, which just means that he is ranked 33rd among the 40 scholastic players. Doobley is number 37, and is paired with another young girl.

Hoobley goes to board 17, and finds that his opponent

has set up the board with some very small plastic pieces. You ask the TD if Hoobley has to play with that set, or can he use his new set. The TD explains that Black has his choice of equipment, and besides Hoobley's set is more standard (he also tells you to put Hoobley's initials on the bottom of each piece, so that you will know they are his). Therefore, the TD tells Charlie that they should use Hoobley's set, and Charlie puts his small set away in its cardboard box.

Charlie does have an analog clock, so they set the clock with both faces at 5:30 so that Charlie and Hoobley will each have 30 minutes to make all their moves (tournament rules require that the clocks be set so that the first time control always expires at 6:00 on analog clocks). Charlie has a scoresheet to keep score, but Hoobley does not know how to write algebraic notation, so he is not keeping score. The TD explains that in some tournaments a TD has the option to make a player who cannot keep score take five minutes off his clock, but that he chooses not do this.

The TD says that he will not start the first round until all the parents are out of the room. You wish Hoobley – and Charlie – good luck and go to the skittles room.

About 10 minutes later Hoobley comes out with a big lower lip. Uh-oh!

"What happened?"

"He checkmated me."

"That was awfully fast."

"Well, he played fast, so I played fast, too. But he kept

taking all my pieces until his Queen and Bishop got in a line and checkmated me."

"Maybe that will be a good lesson. You have plenty of time and all the other kids are still playing, so maybe you should play a little slower, too."

You ask the TD if Hoobley will play his next game soon, but the TD says, "No, in a Swiss system you pair a player against someone who is doing as well as he is, so we have to wait until all the players are done so that we can use the computer to make the next round's pairings. It should be about 11 o'clock. Did your son and his opponent mark down the results of his game on the pairing sheet?"

They hadn't, so he reminds them to do so as soon as each game is over. At the TD's suggestion, you also check to make sure Hoobley has put all of his pieces back into his bag and that Charlie remembers his set and clock. It is only 10:15. So Hoobley and Charlie play another game in the skittles room, and Hoobley plays slower in the skittles game that didn't count than he did in the one that just finished, which did count!

By 10:30 Doobley also comes out. She says she won with something called "Philidor's Legacy." You ask what that is, but her answer about "smothered mate" does not ring a bell.

By 11, all the scholastic players are done and the new pairings posted. Hoobley' is given White on board 16 against a slightly older boy who had also lost. You help Hoobley set up his pieces, set the clock, and then leave the room.

Someone has entered the tournament late, and has missed the first round. So there are now an odd number of players in Hoobley's section. When you saw Hoobley's pairing, at the bottom of the pairing sheet one of the rated players who lost in the first round is given a "bye." You ask the TD what that is. The TD explains that with an odd number of players, one of the players cannot be paired, and any time someone cannot play for any reason that is called a "bye." In this case it is not the player's fault, so he gets a "full-point bye," which is worth the same as a win.

This time, Hoobley does not come out right away. In fact, one other game finishes first before Hoobley comes out. Uh-oh! Big lower lip again!

"I played slower, but I still lost!"

"That's OK – as long as you try your best, that's all you can do."

"I didn't see that he could take my queen."

"Did you mark the result of your game?"

"No – he is marking it."

"The TD said you should both mark it, so why don't you go check?"

Hoobley checks to see that indeed, he has been recorded as lost, and then you take him to lunch, as the next round does not start until 12:30. There will be one more round after that, for a total of four. You should be home by 3.

When you return at 12:20, the pairings are already up, but a note on them says that you cannot start your opponent's clock until 12:30. You also see Doobley, who is chewing on her favorite spinach sandwich, which she brought to the tournament. Apparently she won pretty quickly using a variation on "Legall's Mate" against someone who plays for the local high school. She is now the only unrated with two points.

At 12:30 you help Hoobley set up his pieces (initials under each piece, as you had been told) to play a very young girl, also in her first tournament. It doesn't take too long after you leave for a sheepish looking Hoobley to emerge from the playing room.

"What happened?"

"She didn't know how to get out of check."

"What does that mean?"

"Well, I checked her with my Queen, and she put a bunch of pieces in the way, which I took off." Then I checked her again and she said she didn't know how to get out of check any more, so she resigned. I won!!"

You smile and give Hoobley a big hug. Then you ask him if he had posted his result.

"No! Will they give me a loss if I forget?"

"I don't think so, but you had better go back and post it. Don't forget to put a '1' by your name and a '0' by hers." Hoobley did, and then went off to play in the skittles room.

Later Doobley also emerges. Her game against a local elementary champion had gone down to the wire, but apparently she had won using the "Lucena" or something like that. She is now 3-0, and only one other boy, a local high school junior, had matched her perfect record. They will play in the final round.

After winning in the third round, Hoobley is now "paired up" against an older, higher-rated boy playing in his second tournament. You remind Hoobley to play slow: "Doobley says, 'When you see a good move, look for a better one.' Take your time." You dutifully leave the playing room and the final round action starts.

Luckily, Hoobley does not emerge with the first pair of players to finish, or even second. But his game is the third.

"I was too tired. I missed that when he moved his bishop his rook was attacking my queen. Oh well. Can we wait until Doobley finishes her game?"

"OK, but then we have to go shopping for Aunt Tilly's birthday."

A while later Doobley comes out. You cannot tell if she had won or lost, for she is using her best poker face. Hoobley runs up to her and says, "Well??"

"It was *Zugzwang*," she replies.

"What is 'soog-svang'?"

"Tsoog-tsvang," as she corrects our pronunciation, "It is when I win because he has no good moves to make and has to make a bad one." A smile now grows on Doobley's face. Somehow I think she has a future in this game …

Before we have a chance to leave, the TD announces that all the games are over and he is going to award the trophies.

Imagine our surprise when he announced that Hoobley, although finishing with a 1-3 record, had won the "3rd Un-rated" prize! It is a trophy about a foot high with a chess king on top. We are all flabbergasted. Good thing we hadn't left to get Aunt Tilly's present.

Later that night, with the new trophy on the mantle and Aunt Tilly's present in the closet, you tuck Hoobley into bed.

"Did you have a good time at the tournament?"

"Yes! But I have one question."

"Sure, honey, what is it?"

"Doobley said that she is going to a big kids' tournament in New York next week. Can we go, too?"

4.2.2 Pre-Registration and Registration
The method by which you sign up with the TD to play in his tournament is called "registration." If you register enough days in advance of the tournament (usually by regular mail, unless the TD's web-site can take your entry fee by credit card), this is usually called "pre-registration" since there is

also almost always a registration period just before the tournament, for players that did not pre-register.

The general rule is that larger tournaments encourage pre-registration by offering a discount for early entry (or else later entries are "penalized"). The reasons for this are twofold:

1) It would be impossible for the first round to start on time

if hundreds of players had to register just before the tournament. It takes time to ensure that each registrant is a current federation member (signing up those who are not), determine rating, section, contact information, etc.

2) Pre-registration helps organizers to estimate how much space, how many scoresheets, helpers, etc. are needed to run the tournament. For example, if 80% of the entrants at a national tournament usually take advantage of the discounted early fee, and if 1,600 pre-register, the organizers can estimate that a further 400 will register at the tournament site, and that they need resources to handle a tournament of about 2,000.

As mentioned above, the USCF and CFC allow only members to play in rated events. Here is how USCF explains the only exception to this: "Participants in the Junior Tournament Player program are an exception to the membership requirement and are allowed to participate in rated play in tournaments run at their school which are limited to only players from that school."

Therefore, one of the prime activities during registration is to determine if a registrant is a current USCF member. All USCF memberships are good through the final day of the month. For example, if you join USCF on June 17, 2002 for one year, then your membership is good through June 30, 2003.

If a participant has never been a member of his national federation, or needs to renew, he will be asked to (re-)join in addition to paying the tournament fee. This will require filling out the membership form, which requires more information (such as mailing address for the magazine) than is needed for normal registration, and thus takes a little extra time. Even when one is required to join a federation, registering usually takes less than five minutes. Consider, however, that if 200 people need to register and each takes only two minutes, that is almost seven hours of work! This enormous amount of labor explains why many large tournaments require pre-registration before the first day of play.

Some very large tournaments even have "tiers" of pre-registration periods. For example, in our 2001 PA State Chess Federation Scholastic Championships held on March 10-11, the least expensive registration was until Feb 17, $10 more was required if received between Feb 18 and March 3, and $20 more after that. We don't want the extra money – we set the higher entry fees to encourage early registration so we can get the tournament started on time!

When registering by mail, the following should be included:

❖ Name of registering player (**exactly** as spelled on the registrant's federation membership card)

❖ Name/date of tournament – the organizer may have more than one event for which he is taking registration

❖ Section name (if there is more than one section)

❖ Schedule (if the tournament offers more than one schedule, such as one-day or two-day options)

❖ If it is a scholastic event, usually include your child's school, grade, and/or age.

❖ Any bye rounds (if you know the participant will miss certain rounds for travel, prior commitment, etc.) Tournaments limit the number of bye rounds for which they will give a ½-point bye, so be aware of how this may affect the registrant's prize chances.

❖ Federation membership ID Number (if a member).

❖ Membership expiration date (if a member).

❖ Latest official rating (if none, then "unrated"). The ratings become official periodically – see the section on ratings later in this chapter.

❖ Contact information – phone or, even better, e-mail, in case the organizer has a question.

In addition, if (re-)joining a federation, extra information is needed. For example, the USCF also requires:

❖ Address (for magazine)

❖ Date of birth (to determine eligibility for less expensive scholastic memberships, etc.)

❖ Whether it is a new membership or renewal (and if so, the old USCF ID#). Even if you haven't been a member for many years, your former ID and rating are still correct.

❖ Membership fees. As of January 1, 2001, USCF membership is $13 annually for age 14 and under who select *School Mates* and $20 for under age 19 who select *Chess Life*.

4.2.3 Swiss System, Pairings, and Posting Results
Most scholastic tournaments are held according to the "Swiss" system. In the Swiss system, each player is paired with another player who has (approximately) the same score. So, if it is a seven-round tournament and a player

has lost his first three games ("0-3"), he will be paired with someone else who is 0-3. The other main concepts of a Swiss system are:

❖   A player will not play the same opponent twice.

❖   For color allocation, the director will try to keep the number of each player's games as White and as Black about equal.

❖   Wherever possible, colors will be alternated.

❖   For each score group (such as one loss and no wins after the first round), the upper half of the players will be paired with the lower half.

One advantage of a Swiss system is that it can handle any number of players, which is important, because chess organizers do not know how many players might show up to play in their "open" tournament. Also, everyone plays all the rounds – no one wants to travel to a chess tournament, lose and be eliminated, and have to travel immediately back home.

To figure out the opponent for each player in each round, players are "seeded" according to their official ratings (see the section below explaining ratings). Players who have never played before or have played so recently that their ratings have not yet become official, are paired as "unrated."

This is easily shown by example. Suppose sixteen students show up for a tournament and their ratings are:

1:	1500
2:	1450
3:	1400
4:	1350
5:	1300
6:	1250
7:	1200
8:	1150
9:	1000
10:	950
11:	900
12:	850
13:	800
14:	Unrated "A"
15:	Unrated "B"
16:	Unrated "C"

The numbers on the left are called the "pairing numbers." Once these are established, the TD or computer will "flip a coin" to see who has White on the first board. Suppose the top-rated 1500 wins the flip; the rest of the top players will alternate color and the top of the first half (#1) will play the top of the second half (#9), so #1 has White against #9, #2 will play Black against #10, etc. The entire set of first round pairings:

	White	Black
Board 1	#1	#9
Board 2	#10	#2
Board 3	#3	#11
Board 4	#12	#4
Board 5	#5	#13
Board 6	#14	#6
Board 7	#7	#15
Board 8	#16	#8

The actual pairings will be posted on a "pairing sheet" on the wall, looking very similar to the above chart. In order to figure out a person's board, color, and opponent, first locate the player's name (where it says "#1" above, instead it will literally show player #1's name). Then look to the far left – that will be his board number, usually in a column with the header "Board #" or "Bd". If his name is in the left column he will be White and if in the right column Black. The other name at his board is that of his opponent.

The player should then go to his board (the number is usually taped to the table). If his opponent is already there, he should tell him his name and ask the opponent his, so that he is sure that he is playing the correct person. The player with Black has the choice of equipment, assuming it is standard. If neither player has a clock, they can ask nearby players to borrow one, or can start the game without one. If the game is running late, the TD will give the players a clock later.

Suppose in the first round all the favorites (#1-8) win. Then for the second round, the players that won (players #1 - #8) and the players that lost (players #9 - #16) are put in separate pairing groups, and the same idea, top-half-against-bottom-half of each score group is applied, with colors alternating so that as many players as possible have one White and one Black after two rounds. The resulting pairings:

	White	Black
Board 1	#6	#1
Board 2	#2	#5
Board 3	#8	#3
Board 4	#4	#7
Board 5	#14	#9
Board 6	#10	#13
Board 7	#16	#11
Board 8	#12	#15

Notice that even though #1 would normally play #5 (1-5, 2-6, 3-7, 4-8), this is not the best pairing, since both players had White in the first round and one of them would have to get a second consecutive White. By switching #5 and #6 (which is allowed under many conditions), both players end up with one White and one Black after two rounds.

As the tournament progresses, players tend to "find their level." The best players keep winning and end up playing each other. The worst players keep losing and end up playing each other, too. And players who are close to the middle will win about half their games, winning when "paired down" (against lower-rated players) and losing when "paired up" (against higher-rated players), assuming few upsets.

After the game is over, BOTH players should go back to the pairing chart (the one which told them where they were playing) and mark their result. There are usually separate columns for results on the same row that showed the board numbers. If one player won and the other lost, then the players should mark "1" in the results column next to the winner and "0" in the results column next to the loser. If the  game was a draw, mark "½" next to both players. If one of the players never showed up, then mark "1F" by the player who was there (and you can even circle it, but never circle a result otherwise, since circling indicates a forfeit!) and 0F by the player who was not there. It is very important for both players to mark their results after every round.

If the TD sees that a game is not marked, he has the right to assume that neither player ever showed up and score it as a double-forfeit, which would mean that neither player will be paired for the next round! So even if you lose, it is important to mark your result!

What is a Bye?
A "bye" is easily defined: it is what happens when one does not play a round in a chess tournament! For a variety of reasons, not all players are able to attend or play every round of a tournament. For example, if there are an odd number of players in your section, someone will probably be given a bye.

How Much is a Bye Worth?
Byes can result in any of the three possible chess scores: 0, ½, or 1 point. It depends upon the situation.

When is a Bye worth 1 Point?
In round-robin tournaments, where everyone plays everyone else, the organizers usually invite an even number of players so that there are no byes unless someone gets ill in the middle of the tournament. However, in "open" tournaments where anyone can play, each section may have an odd or even number of players. Without going into the specifics of tournament rules, if there are an odd number of players ready to play, generally the player who has the least number of points with the lowest rating does not get paired and instead may be given a 1-point ("full-point") bye.

How Many 1-Point Byes Can You Get?
Unless there are more rounds than players (rare), a player can only get one 1-point bye per tournament. If a player has missed a round due to a bye, then if there are still an odd number of players, he will play all the remaining rounds.

What About ½-Point Byes?
Many tournament organizers offer ½-point byes for some of the rounds which you know in advance you cannot play.

The main stipulation is that the player has to tell the TD before a specific time, which varies according to each tournament's rules.

Example: The tournament is six rounds and the TD offers ½-point byes for a total of up to two rounds. All ½-point byes for rounds 1-4 have to be requested at least one hour prior to the posted starting time of the round. Requests for a ½-point bye for either rounds 5 or 6 have to be requested before round 4 (to prevent someone who needs a draw to win the tournament from just taking a bye to win).

Do all tournaments offer ½-point byes for rounds you will miss?
Many do, but not all. The bye policy may be stated in the Tournament Life Announcement (TLA) or it may be posted or announced before the first round. Some less important tournaments may offer ½-point byes for all the rounds you cannot play.

What are 0-point byes?
Zero-point byes are given for rounds that a player cannot make, but which do not qualify for a ½-point bye. These are different from forfeits, when a player does NOT tell the TD that he cannot make a round, and is paired but does not show up. Forfeits not only require the TD to withdraw a player from a tournament (not pair him for subsequent rounds), but also may subject the player to a small fine from the organizers next time the player wishes to play in one of their tournaments. Intentional forfeits are considered bad sportsmanship. Both 0-point byes and forfeits are worth 0 points, but after a 0-point bye (or any bye, for that matter), a player continues to be paired until either the tournament is over or he tells the tournament director he is withdrawing from the tournament.

What if you do have to withdraw from the tournament? Are you ineligible for prizes?

If a player has to withdraw from the tournament, or knows that he will not be playing the final N rounds, he should notify the tournament director as soon as he is aware that he will not be playing. The tournament director will then assign the proper bye value to the missed rounds and award the prizes based on his total.

Example: Suppose the tournament is seven rounds and the tournament director offers ½-point byes for a total of up to two rounds, but byes for rounds 6 and 7 have to be requested before round 5. A player has a score of 2-2 and gets ill. He tells the director after his fourth round that he have to leave. The director will give you him two ½-point byes (the maximum) and one 0-point bye. His final score will be 3-4.

Are Byes Rated?

No, byes cannot be rated! A rating system is a scientific method of determining playing performance. Rating an unplayed game is not a measure of performance, so of course byes cannot affect someone's rating.

4.2.5 Ratings and Prizes

Ratings are numerical assignments that measure the playing performance of an individual. The higher the rating, the better the player. Ratings are generally in the range of 100-2800. Here is what the USCF web-site (www.uschess.org) says about ratings:

> "The rating system described here is for over-the-board competition only ... The basic theory of the USCF's rating system is that the difference between the ratings of players is a guide to predicting the outcome of a contest between those two players.

"The specific formula has been worked out according to statistical and probability theory. No rating, however, is a precise evaluation of a player's strength. Instead, ratings are averages of performances and should be viewed as approximations within a range ..."

USCF Rating Classification

Senior Master	above 2399
Master	2200-2399
Expert	2000-2199
Class A	1800-1999
Class B	1600-1799
Class C	1400-1599
Class D	1200-1399
Class E	1000-1199
Class F	800- 999
Class G	600- 799
Class H	400- 599
Class I	200- 399

There is a new rating algorithm which is somewhat more complicated than the old system, but it is outside the scope of this book (see www.uschess.org/ratings/info/system.html). Suffice it to say that when one wins, his rating goes up, and when one loses, his rating goes down. The higher the rating of the opponent beaten, the more it goes up; the lower the rating of the opponent lost to, the more it goes down.

It takes four games (lifetime, not per tournament) to get a published rating. USCF publishes the ratings on the web at www.64.com/uscf/ratings and the CFC at www.chess.ca/ratings.htm. In the US, if one has played less than 25 games, his rating is considered "provisional" and is less accurate than the ratings of those who have played 25 games or more.

In many tournaments, ratings are used to determine eligibility for prizes. For example, in the Rating Classification Table above, each rating is part of a "class." It is easy to use these classes for prize eligibility. For example, one might have a scholastic tournament and give out prizes for the Top Three overall finishers, plus for the Top Two finishers in Class D, Class E, and Class F. Or, if you want to include multiple classes in one prize, such as for "Class F and Below," this is often advertised as an "Under-1000" prize, because everyone with a rating under 1000 is eligible, as opposed to a "Class F prize," where only players in the range 800-999 should be eligible.

 If multiple players who are eligible for the same prize should end the tournament with the same number of points, and the prize is indivisible (like a trophy), then *tiebreaks* are used to determine the prize. Tiebreaks usually involve "strength of opposition" – the player who has played opponents who have done the best in that tournament have the highest tiebreaks. For example, the usual "first tiebreak" in USCF tournaments is "Modified Median," which adds up the final scores of all your opponents (except one or two, as specified by the rule). So a player who plays several opponents who did very well will have a higher modified median tiebreak than one who played opponents who did not do as well.

While the USCF has the oldest rating system, other scholastic organizations (CFC, CEA, Chess'n Math, etc.) all have independent systems that are similar, based on results in their non-USCF tournaments.

One final important thing about ratings – don't get too carried away with them. In fact, most students should forget their rating and that of their opponent, and just play as much chess as they can against anyone. Players who start worrying more about their rating than about learning don't improve nearly as fast as those who concentrate on learning.

One does not get a good rating by worrying about his rating and "protecting" it by playing only certain players. One gains a better rating by seeking out the strongest opponents (but not ducking the weaker ones) and playing and learning as much as you can.

4.2.6 The Skittles Room

The "skittles" room is usually located somewhere outside, but near, the tournament room. It is where one may go after the game is over and when awaiting the pairings for the next round. By some definitions, "skittles" is chess for fun, or chess played without a clock – so a skittles room is, by definition, not a place for serious chess.

Unlike the tournament room, which is kept quiet, the skittles room is usually very noisy. Anyone is allowed in the skittles room, and many players go there after their games to analyze them with their opponents (the so-called "post-mortem"; one can learn a lot that way!).

At large tournaments, the skittles room (or a nearby area) often features a chess bookseller, who also sells chess equipment, videos, t-shirts, etc. Other skittles areas might sell food.

4.2.7 Enhancing Your Tournament Experience

So your child is going to a live chess tournament! Congratulations – it will be fun. Here are some tips to enhance his – and your – experience:

1. Register by mail ahead of time – This is allowed in most tournaments and serves several purposes. It helps the tournament director get the first round started on time, and also gives him time to check your registration information more thoroughly. It also usually entitles you to a discount. While almost all tournaments allow you to register on the same day as the first round (and by all means if you need to wait until then, please do and register then – most registrants do), "pre-registration" lets you sleep a little later. If you do pre-register, make sure you check your registration when you get to the tournament, no less than 15-30 minutes before the first round is scheduled. <u>One exception</u>: If you are joining your federation for the first time and it is a small tournament, it is easier to join at the tournament, since you will need to supply additional information over and above that needed for normal pre-registration. Make sure all your registration information is clear, complete, and correct as described in Section 4.2.2.

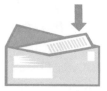

2. Have your child get plenty of sleep. Playing chess correctly is fun, but tiring – there is a lot of mental work required, like taking a test! A well-rested player is a much better player.

3. Know the directions to the tournament location and give yourself a little extra time – no sense missing the first round because of a traffic jam, a detour, etc.

4. Bring chess equipment! Except for national tournaments, most tournaments do not supply anything but scoresheets. So bring a standard Staunton chess set and board, a chess clock (if you have one), and a couple of pencils/pens to record your games (if you know how).

 **Please put your name and contact information on the back of your board, your name on your clock, and your initials on the bottom of each chess piece.**
Many players have similar pieces and boards, and if yours are lost or left somewhere too long, it helps tremendously to have them labeled. It is a good idea to purchase a scorebook, with many bound scoresheets, to save your recorded games for later study.

5. Learn ahead of time how to set and use your chess clock. If it is a digital clock, read the instructions and set the clock in advance to the time limit advertised for your tournament. For example, if the time limit is "G/30" that means play all your moves in 30 minutes. If that includes a standard time delay of 5 seconds per move, then the clock is set at "G/25; T/D 5" meaning it counts down from 25 minutes to zero on each side of the clock and the clock is set to delay five seconds before each move. If you purchased an analog clock, then it cannot use time delay, so G/30 simply means each player has 30 minutes, so set each face of the clock to 5:30, since the first time control should always expire at 6:00.

6. Have your child learn algebraic notation (this is taught in almost every beginner's book) so he can keep score and go over his games later. Tournament rules require everyone who knows how to keep score during a rated game until at least one of the players has less than five minutes left, so older kids will be expected to do so, anyway. It also helps them during any disputes over the game, providing a "proof of record" that the TD can use. Here is algebraic notation for "Scholar's Mate":

White	Black
1. e4	e5
2. Qh5	Nc6
3. Bc4	Nf6??
4. Qxf7#	

7. Make sure to check the date/time of registration and the times of the rounds. Tournament information is posted at www.uschess.org/tla, www.chess.ca/tournaments.htm, and elsewhere. If you must, call or e-mail the TD or registration person to confirm needed information. For multiple-day tournaments be aware that *rounds may start on different times on different days*!

If your child is joining the federation, fill out a membership form – in the US, the less expensive membership includes the children's *School Mates* Magazine and the more expensive membership (required for students over the age of 14) entitles them to the adult *Chess Life*. Keep a copy of the "member's" form – it will be your proof of membership at other tournaments until you get your membership card in a few weeks. If you cannot prove current membership at a tournament, the TD may require you to join for an additional year – he cannot let you play without proof (which can be your membership card, your membership form copy, your magazine mailing label, or a copy of your membership information as printed out from the web-site ratings page).

8. Help your child learn to find his pairing after the pairing sheet is posted. His board number will be on the extreme left. The left-hand name will play White and the right-hand name will play Black. Play will start when the TD says to start the clocks, usually about the time posted for the round.

After the first round starts, the TD will post a "Wall Chart" with your child's name, membership ID, and rating. Double-check these to make sure they are correct – if not, notify the TD immediately. At a recent tournament one player told me AFTER I GAVE OUT THE TROPHIES that his rating was incorrect and he should have won a trophy. He had two days to tell me, and his rating had been posted the entire time, but he waited until after the tournament was over. Too late. Please let the TD know ASAP ...

9. Bring a small snack to eat during long games – most tournaments allow players to eat quietly (no chips!) during a game, and it is important not to get too hungry.

10. During the game, if there is any question at all, teach your child to stop his game and GET THE TOUR-NAMENT DIRECTOR. I have seen dozens of cases where even experienced tournament players "decide" how to solve a problem incorrectly, always to the detriment of one of the players. When in doubt, your child should stop his clock and get the TD.

11. Etiquette – teach your child the following: before the game, introduce yourself to your opponent to make sure you are playing the correct person. Shake hands before Black starts the clock to begin the game.

During the game, limit talking to such things as "Would you like a draw?" or "That is an illegal move" or "You touched that piece, you have to move it." A player may say "check," but it is not necessary, and against strong  opponents it is considered an insult (they know it is check). If a player is in a hopeless position, he may resign by saying "I resign" or purposely turning down his king (resigning is proper, but you should instruct your child never to resign to a beginner who might not know how to finish the game with checkmate!). If you need to adjust a piece that has fallen down or is not centered, do so on your time, but before you do, say "I adjust" or "j'adoube." More on etiquette in Section 4.5.

12. After the game, BOTH players, win or lose, must report their result by putting a "1" next to the winner and a "0" next to the loser (or ½ by each in the case of a draw) on the pairing sheet. If the result is not reported, the TD may assume that the game was not played, it was a double-forfeit and that both players went home. Therefore, they may not be paired for the next round. So mark your results, win or lose!

13. If your child has to leave (whether you are coming back or not) and will miss a round (or more) or is withdrawing, you should one, notify the TD as soon as you are aware of this, and two, also remind the TD at the time you leave (and when you come back, if applicable).

14. Tell the tournament director what you liked about the tournament and, constructively, what might have worked better – he will appreciate both your consideration and your comments!

4.3 Common Misconceptions About Tournaments and Scholastic Chess

Misconception: Parents often think their child is not good enough to play in tournaments, or "Tournaments are just for the kids that are really good."

Fact: There is no minimum skill level required. Participants do have to know how the pieces move and the rules, like checkmate! They also have to be able to play quietly.

Misconception: Parents think their child will go to a tournament, lose in the first round, be eliminated, and go home disconsolate.

Fact: No one is eliminated from Swiss tournaments, which are how almost all scholastic tournaments are held. Swiss tournaments were explained above in Section 4.2.3. Even other types of tournament formats, like round-robins, do not eliminate players.

Misconception: You have to pre-register (register before the day of the tournament) to play in a tournament.

Fact: While pre-registration is encouraged and is often less expensive, most entries for small and mid-sized tournaments are made during a registration period just prior to play on the day of the tournament.

Misconception: You have to play all the rounds in a tournament in order to participate (this is a very common misconception).

Fact: Of course, no one forces you to play all the rounds. If you do plan on leaving, please notifying the tournament director about when you plan to leave (and come back) and then notify him each time you do.

Misconception: Tournaments will provide a board and set for every participant.

Fact: Few tournaments provide equipment (except for scoresheets)! So at least bring a set, board, and pencil. The exceptions would be the big national tournaments, which supply boards and sets, but not clocks. At the end of the tournament, these "used" and specially designated boards (with the name of the tournament on them) are usually sold, along with the sets, at a slight discount.

Misconception: Younger students shouldn't or can't play in clubs or tournaments with adults.
Fact: Many students play regularly in tournaments with adults, and sometimes beat them!

Misconception: Most tournaments have age or residency restrictions.
Fact: Most tournaments are open to anyone; tournaments just for students are restricted to "scholastic" players, which means grades 12 or below. There are rarely residence restrictions.

Misconception: You have to have a rating to play in a tournament.
Fact: The USCF requires membership to play in their rated tournaments. Therefore, everyone starts his first tournament as "unrated" – it is impossible to get an official USCF rating before playing in a tournament, so that would be a Catch-22! And you don't have to be a member before registration – you can always join as part of registration.

Misconception: A player who has not played in a long time loses his rating, or his rating decreases.
Fact: The USCF has a slogan "Once rated, always rated." And when you don't play, your rating does not change.

4.4 Tournament Rules
With a few exceptions (en passant, promotion, castling,

draws), most non-tournament players know the rules involving the moves of the pieces about as well as tournament players do. However, when playing in tournaments, there are a few other pertinent rules that are good to know, especially those involving the clock and scorekeeping. Some of these rules are covered elsewhere in this book under their respective topics. I devote an entire chapter of *Everyone's 2nd Chess Book* to this but, because of their importance, the most common are summarized below.

The USCF's *Official Rules of Chess* runs several hundred pages, but nobody expects a player to know them all, or even most of them. But there is one rule every player must know: If anything strange, unusual, or misunderstood is happening at your board, or if you have a dispute with your opponent, **you have the right to – and should – stop your clock and ask a TD a question or make a "claim."** The TD cannot answer general questions like "Is this checkmate?" or educate you about various drawing options during a game, but he can explain any rule you ask, and will determine the proper action if something you don't understand is brought to his attention. This rule about contacting the TD is VERY IMPORTANT, so teach your child to stop his game, get the TD (or raise his hand, if that is what the TD instructed), and say "*I have a question.*" or "*I would like to make a claim.*". Examples of claims are "Illegal move" or "Draw by three-fold repetition." At every

scholastic tournament the results of several games are affected because a player believes something his opponent says or fails to contact the TD. So when in doubt – stop the game and get the TD!

1. Chess is played with a clock:

❖ The clock has two faces, and only one face runs at a time. After each player moves, he hits his side of the clock to stop it from running and start his opponent's side. In a "sudden death" time control (where all the moves must be made within a specific amount of time on the clock; this is how almost all scholastic events are held), if a player runs out of time (usually indicated on a digital clock by "0:00", or on an analog clock by a "flag" falling) and the opponent calls it before his time runs out as well, then if the opponent has any possible mating material, such as a pawn or a Rook, the opponent wins the game. If the opponent does not have mating material, it is a draw.

 ❖   If neither player has a clock, and they cannot easily borrow one, they can start their game without a clock. If the game is running long, the TD will find a clock and give it to them, splitting the remaining time in the round equally between the two players.

❖   The accepted standard for a USCF game is to use a digital clock with a *time-delay* feature. A time-delay means the clock does not run for a certain number of seconds (usually 5 seconds in a longer tournament game) after it is pressed. This delay allows completion of extremely long games in sudden death time limits, as a player can play indefinitely without his clock running out, so long as he takes less than 5 seconds per move. Usually if a clock has time delay on, the TD requires that the first time control be shortened proportionately, so that the entire session takes about the same time. For example, if the session is "Game in 30 minutes," then with a 5-second time delay, each player would start with 25 minutes, but still the game should take about one hour, the same as a game played without the time delay feature.

2. If You Know How to Record Your Game, Then You Must

In a tournament, if a player knows how to keep score, he must. If he does not know how, he can't. However, most players above the age of 8 are expected to learn algebraic notation quickly. This rule is sometimes altered for young players; for example, some TDs subtract five minutes from the clock for players who do not know how to keep score, so you may wish to check with the TD at the start of the tournament to see how he is enforcing this rule. Note that chess scorekeeping does not depend on having correctly recorded previous moves, so if someone messes up his score, that is not an excuse to stop. A player also has the right to request an opponent's scoresheet so long as the player borrowing the scoresheet does so while his clock is running. Both players may stop keeping score when *either* player gets to five minutes or less left on his clock.

3. Avoiding Spectator Interference

If parents or coaches are allowed to spectate, they should do so from behind their child or student, so that body lan-

guage is not an issue. Even if they see illegal moves, they should not interfere. One way to look at it is that spectators should not do anything a wall wouldn't do! Chess is a game *between the two players*. Under certain conditions, the rules allow the TD to interfere, but in no case may another party interfere with the players. The only time an outside party should say something is if he observes the type of cheating by a player which his opponent could not possibly have seen (such as secretly using a computer). This should be reported to the TD immediately. Even after a player calls a TD in for a question, coaches or parents should not interfere or act as a "lawyer" for their player. If the TD wishes to use them as a witness, the TD may do so. Guidelines for spectator conduct are presented in Appendix B.

4. Touch Move

❖ If you touch a piece you must move it.

❖ If you take your hand off your piece you must leave it there.

❖ If you touch or purposely displace an opponent's piece and you can capture it, you must.

5. Types of Draws (* = Automatic; others must be claimed before the player presses his clock)

❖ <u>Three-fold repetition of position</u> (NOT 3-fold repetition of moves). There is no "perpetual check" draw, but it always leads to a three-fold repetition.

❖ <u>Insufficient Mating Material</u>* (Just a King, King and Bishop, King and Knight, or King and Two Knights)

❖ <u>Stalemate</u>* – The side to move is not in check and NONE of his pieces can make a legal move.

❖ <u>Agreement</u> – One player makes a move, offers a draw, and hits his clock. If the opponent agrees before making a responding move, the game is a draw.

❖ <u>50-move Rule</u> – If at any time during the game *both* players complete *50 consecutive moves* without a pawn being moved or any piece being captured.

❖ <u>Both Players Run Out of Time</u> – If both players run out of time, and neither had claimed a win before his time ran out, the game is declared a draw.

❖   <u>Insufficient Losing Chances</u> – Allows a player with less than five minutes left and without a time-delay clock to claim a draw if he is clearly not losing, but thinks he might lose on time if he continues playing for a win or draw.

4.5 Tournament Etiquette

Players

For the most part, chess is played on the honor system, since outside of international events, there are usually many more tournament players than TDs at an event. So the #1 rule is that if there is anything unusual happening at your board, get the TD. The most important etiquette rule is that a player may not disturb his opponent, but since what disturbs a person varies widely, it is up to each player to let the TD know if something is bothering him.

Similarly, it is not bad sportsmanship if a player points out that his opponent has made an illegal move, or has touched a piece and has to move it. On the contrary, this is expected of all chess players, and players who do not insist that their opponent follow the rules are at a definite disadvantage.

Declaring "check" is sometimes considered rude, especially outside of beginner play. The reason is that all good players know it is check, so saying check may be like saying "You may not be good enough to realize this, so I will tell you." Therefore, the rules discourage, but do not forbid one from saying "check."

Good sportsmanship usually requires you to shake hands and identify yourself at the start of a game, and to shake hands and say something like "thanks" or "good game" at the end. It is also worth noting that shaking hands does **not** end a game, but you should not shake hands unless you agree that the game is over; doing so otherwise may lead to arguments. The correct way to resign is to say "I resign" or purposely tip over your king.

Spectators

This can be easily summarized. Spectators should do their best imitation of a wall! See Appendix B for a complete set of rules.

A lot of adults think if they stand by quietly that probably has no effect. Unfortunately, an adult can easily intimidate a child's young opponent just by standing next to the game. While tournament rules require such an interested spectator to stand behind his child or student, so as to not give inadvertent information via body language, that position still may result in upsetting the opponent. Therefore, I forbid parents from even being in the room for championship scholastic events, and non-championship ones that involve young children. At national events involving young scholastic players, it is standard procedure that only the tournament directors and other approved spectators be allowed in the playing room.

As an example, I once held a small, unrated prize tournament in one of my beginner classes. While I had taught my students to stop the game if anything unusual happened, neither of the young participants remembered this when they got into a heated battle. Just as the clock on both player's sides were getting low, one of the players made an illegal move, moving into check. The other player did not see this, but since they were playing for prizes, I did not intervene (by the way, in events where tournament directors cannot watch all the games, the TD has the right to stop the game in this circumstance, but since he cannot do so in all cases fairly, he may simply refrain from doing so and act as a witness, as I was doing).

Just then, one of the fathers arrived to pick up his son, one of the participants in this game. He looked at the illegal position and immediately started protesting that allowing such play was not right. I tried to tell the irate parent that he was interfering with the game and that it was up to the players to decide the game, and that the participants would need to call for intervention, as they had been taught, but which had not happened.

To make a long story short, the father refused to stop protesting and I had to stop the game, declaring it a draw because the father was not only disturbing the players, but profoundly affecting the result.

4.6 Important Scholastic Tournament and Titles

This section addresses local, state, national, and international tournaments for scholastic players. There are a number of annual events at each level that enable students to earn titles which they will cherish – and even might help them when they apply for admission to college!

Local Tournaments

Aside from the "TD Tom special" local tournaments found on many weekends, many areas which feature strong chess organizations, such as active USCF affiliates and clubs, sponsor local championships. These championships might be for your town, city, county, or even a larger region. Clever organizers should make as much use as they can of these titles, as that allows many different titles to be awarded.

For example, in the Philadelphia area, we could have the Greater Philadelphia Open Scholastic Championship, the Greater Philadelphia Scholastic Invitational Championship (where only the highest-rated players are invited to play), a Greater Philadelphia Junior Championship (for players

Under age 19, including some that may be in college), and other tournaments with a wider geographic scope, such as a Delaware Valley Scholastic Championship or a South-eastern PA Scholastic Championship. We don't do all of these because it takes a lot of organization to run so many championship events, but some areas do feature many such local tournaments, and then there are plenty of titles to go around!

Furthermore, within each tournament there are multiple champions. There can be champions based on age, grade, school level, or rating class, for example:

❖ Greater Philadelphia Under-10 Champion;
❖ Greater Philadelphia 7th grade Champion;
❖ Greater Philadelphia Middle School Champion; or
❖ Greater Philadelphia Under-1400 Scholastic Champion

State and Province Championships
Each state has a state chess federation (California has two: Northern and Southern) that is the state's official arm of the USCF. These state chess federations usually host an annual state scholastic chess championship, often in late winter or early spring. The scholastic chess championships are usually held as separate events from the adult "State Championship," though a small state might consider combining these events.

At the scholastic state/province championships the annual titles are awarded to the winners in various scholastic categories, similar to those discussed in the previous section. So if someone you meet says he knows the state Middle School Champion, that title was won at your state's scholastic championship. These tournaments are almost always open, which means that anyone can play; participants don't have to qualify or be "good" players.

Sometimes this difference between chess and other more well known sports leads to confusion. For example, if Pete Sampras plays for the Wimbledon title, that usually means he was good enough to be invited to the tournament and at least make it to the final. But if Sammy Down-the-Street plays "for the state scholastic championship" he may not even know much more than how to move the pieces! So Sammy may not be the state scholastic champion, but he certainly did compete for it!

In 1967 Pennsylvania reinstated its Scholastic Champion- ship and in 1968 I played and finished sec- ond in the high school division. As a strong tournament player, I was aware of all of the subsequent PA High School Champi- ons during the next several years – I knew  all of them personally. Yet when some friends and acquain- tances found out that I was a strong chess player, they often told me, "I knew a kid who was the state High School Champion." But in no case had that person ever won the PA High School Championship! Obviously the confusion stemmed from the "whisper-down-the-lane" aspect of hav- ing an open tournament where anyone can play "for the championship" and the fact that each year out of the hun- dreds who may compete, only one can win the title.

National Scholastic Championships
The USCF and CFC sponsor several annual national events that are open to any young player. For example the USCF offers:

❖   National High School Championship – determines the National HS Champion

❖ National Jr. High Championship – Determines the National Junior High (K-9) and Middle School (K-8) Champions

❖ National Elementary Championship – Determines the National Elementary (K-6 and K-5) Champions and the National Primary (K-3) Champion

❖ National Scholastic K-12 Grade Championship – Determines the National Champion for each grade.

❖ U.S. Junior Chess Congress – Open to all players under age 19

❖ US Junior Open – Open to all players under age 21 – Determines US Jr. Open Champion

In years like 2001, when the High School, Jr. High, and Elementary are played at the same time and place, that combined tournament has been designated a "SuperNational." At these gigantic events *several thousand* students from all over the US participate! The 2001 event in Kansas City drew about 4,700 participants, making it the largest chess tournament ever held in the US.

National tournaments are held in a different location each year, with cities submitting competitive bids to become the host. One can find detailed information on each year's event by going to your federation's web-site. There may be one near you this year, or you may want to plan on traveling to one, just for the fun of it. For example, the US 2000 K-12 was in Orlando, so it was a good chance for the parents to visit Disney World – with or without the young chess player!

In addition to these open events, there are several "closed" invitational events that are held to determine national champions. The oldest example is the US Junior Championship, which was revived in 1966 and has been running annually ever since.

The *Chess Education Association* (CEA) holds their own CEA Grand National Scholastic Chess Championship and their Annual All America Cup.

The CFC runs their "Canadian Youth Chess Championships." These championships are part of an international program, the World Youth Chess Championships, run by FIDE. The Canadian national scholastic championship is called the Canadian Chess Challenge. It has been organized by the *Chess'n Math Association* since its inception 13 years ago. Competition is in four stages: school, regional, provincial, and national. The North American Chess Challenge, is an international scholastic tournament run by *Chess'n Math* in the United States each year.

International Scholastic Events
At the international level, most of the events are "invitational," that is, the USCF and CFC invite their top-rated  players who qualify to represent their country at that event. For example, the US and Canada might each have one or two representatives invited to the World Junior Championship. Using a preset formula based on ratings and other factors, the federation calculates who the top candidates are. If a player is unable to attend, then they invite the next in line, until the federation has filled all of its positions.

However, many of these events have age restrictions, so not just the top-rated players are invited. The World Youth Championships has multiple sections by age and gender, such as Boys Under-16 and Girls Under-10. For example, Alisa Melekhina, one of the top-rated elementary school students in Philadelphia, and at this writing the country's fourth-rated nine-year-old girl, got a chance to represent the US at that tournament late in 2000 (by the way, Alisa did very well in her first international competition, scoring six of 11 points for 17th place! And in 2002, she improved to 4th!).

Besides World Championships, there are also championships of continents or hemispheres. In 2000 Noah Belcher of New York became the "Pan-Am" champion for his age group by representing the US in Brazil and winning his section. The next year Alisa Melekhina did the same. There are European and Asian Championships as well.

There are also international team tournaments, where groups of four represent their countries. The most famous is the World Student Team Championship. In this case most of the players are college students, as the definition of "student" extends beyond scholastic, and so many of the best players in the world are eligible.

If a player performs well enough in these events, he or she gets a FIDE (international) rating and maybe even a FIDE title. You may have heard of these, which are, in ascending order: FIDE Master (FM), International Master (IM), and International Grandmaster (GM).

So if your child aspires to the highest title, Grandmaster, tell him he will have to work his way up the ladder and do extremely well in international chess events. Becoming a Grandmaster always takes many years of difficult study and play, so we wish him or her good luck!

Chapter 5

The Road to Improvement

5.1 Identifying Individual Needs

Beginners in chess, as in most similar endeavors, are not very skillful. Their initial capability varies widely according to age and nature. A beginning chess player does not have the experience to recognize the recurring patterns that are necessary for competent play; that comes with time and practice. So his skills need to be nurtured if he is to progress.

Each child feels differently about the need to improve. Those who find the game dull or uninteresting will likely not wish to get better at all. Even those who fall in love with the game differ greatly in their desire to improve. Among those eager to improve, some wish to do so with a minimum of work, while others understand that you get out what you put in. Almost any player who wants to become really proficient will have to put in a fair amount of work. A saying goes "Chess: an hour to learn, a lifetime to master." In this sense chess is like many other complex activities, like playing baseball or the piano.

So many youngsters never find the urge to improve at chess or feel the need to work at it – and that is certainly natural and acceptable. But many parents who are reading this book likely have enthusiastic young chess players who are looking to improve. This chapter should help you get them started.

All young chess players love to play, but can be divided into two groups: 1) youngsters that *only* like to play, and 2) those that also like to read chess books, watch chess videos, solve chess problems, etc.

If your child only likes to play, that is fine! In fact, students who believe that studying chess is work, not fun, are probably in the great majority of young players. You may have a mental picture of the stereotypical chess student, locking himself in his room reading chess books, but though they usually turn out to be some of the best players, these "chess work is fun" students, like Josh Waitzkin in *Searching for Bobby Fischer*, are relatively rare. Students who do not wish to study problems and famous games are much more common. These students should slowly improve as they play more games, and will do so somewhat quicker if they at least attempt to recognize their mistakes and try to minimize repeating them in future play. The remainder of this section addresses the student who *likes* to study chess.

Like becoming good at anything else, chess requires both theory and practice to make steady progress. Practice involves playing, while theory might mean studying books or videos, or taking lessons. The main part of theory is to study chess concepts at home on a steady basis; the other part is instruction (see Section 5.3). For example, in 11th and 12th grade I spent about 5 to 10 times as much time studying chess as I did on schoolwork – and I was my class valedictorian! But I never expect my students to be as gung-ho as I was – I thought all that chess "work" was fun!

For all beginners, there are two things you must do at home to make progress. The first is to play at least two slow games a week. Students age 8 or older should learn to record their games so they can study every game they play (if the game is slow enough – see below). Having a record of the game allows them to review their play, which is an important part of improvement.

Recording requires a student to write down each move *for both players*. At first recording may seem like a burden, but this feeling will quickly disappear if the student practices for several hundred moves (about 7 games for each color) in a short period of time. Recording about five or six games in a week's time is effective, at least until the effort is hardly noticeable. Since recording with White is slightly easier than with Black, the student should initially play White in all the games where scorekeeping is practiced. Once recording with White seems easy, then all the games should be played as Black until that also seems easy.

Ready-made scoresheets and scorebooks are available for recording. It is a good idea before each game to fill out the information at the top of the scoresheet: who played White and Black, the date, the time control for the game ("none" if not played with a clock), etc. If possible, a student should record every game he plays when there is either no clock (skittles) or when he has at least half an hour on the clock (Game/30 or slower).

In my experience, a student who plays less than one game a week tends to regress; more than one game a week is necessary for progress. For students who love to play  chess, it should not be a problem to average two games a week – he can play against his dog or the wall, if necessary. However today, with computers and the Internet providing ready opponents, it should be relatively easy to find an opponent. A good minimum would be to spend at least an hour or two per week playing a couple of games.

The second part of the homework is to do tactical problems from a tactics book. Tactics are the most important part of chess – especially for beginners. I suggest that beginning students start with John Bain's book *Chess Tactics for Students,* which features basic tactical motifs – I recommend these over checkmate books since tactical motifs occur on a high percentage of moves, while checkmates occur less frequently. Bain also has a checkmate book, or the student can try *Bobby Fischer Teaches Chess.* Even students initally reluctant to study may find doing these problems is fun!

A student should do as many of these problems as he can each week (hiding all the clues unless he needs them; just read the "White to play" or "Black to play" part). Some of my students even finish an entire book in the first few weeks (!). At a minimum a student should do at least a few problems every week, and then when finished, should repeat the book until he can solve almost all of the problems quickly. The student should not spend a lot of time doing a problem – no more than about five minutes. If he does not solve the problem, he should look in the answer section for the solution. The goal is to *get the pattern into his memory*, not to prove that he can solve the problem in a few hours. A student should try *not* to set up a board and move the pieces. After all, in a real chess game, a player does not get to move the pieces to analyze, so it is a good idea not to move the pieces in practice. However, if the student does not understand – or cannot visualize – the answer, then by all means get out a set and play it out until there is recognition of why that answer works; if there is still a problem, ask a stronger player or give the problem to the computer!

Like learning multiplication tables, the repetition of these basic chess patterns, until they are quickly recognizable, will form a strong basis for improvement in chess!

One of the problems with studying by yourself is deciding which of the thousands of chess books are right for you, given your level of proficiency. In fact, many players, both adults and students, make the mistake of studying the wrong books, spending lots of time but showing little improvement. That is a major reason for getting some strong coaching. That option will be covered next.

5.3 Instruction

The Best Instructor for Your Child
If your child does wish instruction, there are two main issues: how to find potential instructors, and how to tell which one is right for your child. If you saw *Searching for Bobby Fischer*, you know how important this process can be.

You might think of chess instructors as being available in three levels: a local friend or teacher, a member of a local chess club, or a professional instructor (usually expert or master level or above).

I offer the following rule of thumb for how  proficient at chess an instructor has to be: when your child is still a beginner, then most experienced tournament players or decent club players (rated 1300-1500) can help him get the basics down. But once your child starts to get serious and is one of the better players for his age in your area, I would suggest that his instructor be rated at least 1700 (Expert starts at 2000 and master at 2200). The reason is that weaker instructors are more likely to allow, or even encourage, unwittingly, bad habits that your child may later find hard to break.

It should not be hard locating a teacher who runs a club at

your child's school (or one close by) who can help your child learn most of the rules. Usually these instructors have never heard of the USCF and don't have a rating. Many of these helpers sometimes do not fully understand such rules as en passant or that you can get multiple queens upon promotion. Also, they may be very weak players who will let your child get into bad habits, or worse, may inadvertently provide misguided instruction.

Many of the above problems can be avoided by looking for help at local chess clubs (see Section 2.6). There are usually competent players at a local club who can probably provide free and kind help. Their knowledge of the rules and guidelines should be adequate.

However, like most things in life, you tend to get what you pay for, and in chess al-most all the best instructors charge for their  time and likely teach chess for a living. Besides generally providing the highest level of instruction, they also usually have the most experience dealing with young-sters of all capabilities. Please note that not all professional instructors are good; many strong play-ers offer paid lessons but are not good teachers. The sug-gestions below will help you find one.

If you do choose to seek out a professional instructor, first ask yourself, "Do the lessons have to be live, or can we do them over the Internet?" There are several pros and cons:

Internet lessons are usually more flexible since you don't have to travel, nor possibly pay extra for an instructor to visit your home.

In-person lessons are, on average, more effective, since your child gets the full benefit of the instructor's body language, tone of voice, etc., and the instructor can show your child supporting information, like what a particular book or chess video looks like, or how to fill out a scoresheet. Of course, one advantage of this method is that "live" lessons do not require a computer with Internet access!

Internet lessons may have hidden charges if your child simultaneously talks with the instructor on the phone or you have to pay for extra web access time. And your (or your instructor's) Internet Service Provider or computer may occasionally have technical difficulties and you may not be able to get access when you want it.

Internet lessons offer a much wider range of really good (and bad) instructors. Unless you live near a major chess center, the better instructors on the Internet are probably much more competent than your local instructors. These are the main factors in deciding whether to use a live or Internet-based instructor.

Another key point in choosing an instructor is that a higher rating does not necessarily make for a better teacher, just as a higher IQ does not necessarily make for a better college professor. Some top-notch players teach because they are great teachers, but others teach just because scholastic chess is becoming a big business and they can make a living that way. They may be good players, but not very good teachers. While the analogy is not perfect, think of a chess instructor like a boxing trainer – just because Mike Tyson was a great fighter does not necessarily mean he would be the best boxing coach for you, and it is well known that the best baseball players did not always make the best managers. Similarly, some lower-echelon masters and experts are wonderful teachers while others are weaker players *and* bad teachers.

There is no sure way to tell ahead of time who will be a

great instructor for your son. Therefore, you might wish to ask for references from students who are similar in age and/or ability – a good teacher should be able to supply you with these without much trouble.

Besides chess ability, what are some attributes of a good instructor? A good instructor:

❖   Has good communication skills, including listening and talking. If he cannot listen well to you when you are deciding whether to hire him, what makes you think he will listen well to your child when he has a question?

❖   Can constructively criticize your child's play without having your child take it personally (some children – and adults! – are very sensitive, and this can sometimes be a concern).

❖   Is able to recognize weaknesses and come up with a homework/study plan to address those weaknesses.

❖   Does not just provide "canned" lessons – he tailors the lessons to your child's needs, and looks over your child's games to see how lessons from previous sessions are being incorporated.

❖   Takes a personal interest in your child. Any good instructor wants his students to learn happily and do well, and not just make sure he gets paid.

❖   Is able to match parent and student goals. A laid-back instructor may not be the best for a go-go student and parent; similarly, a very aggressive instructor may not match

 a parent who is looking for a "fun" instructor who de-emphasizes competition.

Similarly, teaching method is important. I generally use the Socratic method, whereby I do not give my students the answer to a question (if I think they know it) but rather lead them through other questions (or hints) to help them figure it out for themselves. This is in accordance with the  philosophy "if you give someone a fish, he eats supper, but if you teach him how to fish he can eat forever." But occasionally some find it frustrating, and even if I know they well know the answer, they give up and say, "Just tell me the answer." Of course, if they are *always* that way, I have to adjust my normal teaching method.

A good sense of humor is not required, but very helpful. Any time there is a potentially long-term relationship, it is nice that your instructor has a lighter side and understands that chess may be more serious for him than it is for you and your child.

The final three items fall into the "chemistry" category. Sometimes there is just a good chemistry between instructor and family. I have been teaching long enough that I have run into families that think I am the best thing since sliced bread or (much more rarely, thank goodness) others that didn't like my sense of humor or my Socratic teaching method and just could not get in sync.

Locating an Instructor
You are probably aware that the Yellow Pages are not the best place to find a chess instructor, although occasionally some are there. In Section 2.4 we discussed how to find clubs; if you are looking for a "live" instructor, contacting one or two local clubs will usually get you a recom-

mendation. Or if that fails you can contact your state affiliate; their contact information is at www.uschess.org/directories/states.html. Once you decide to use "outside" instruction, then your options widen considerably. Federation magazines have ads for instruction in their classified sections, and many web-sites feature a list of instructors, like the Internet Chess Club at www.chessclub.com, Chess Links at www.chesslinks.org/scholastic/index.html, or Chessopolis at www.chessopolis.com.

Chess Lessons and Fun

Ideally, chess lessons should always be fun. After all, chess is a fun game, students perceive that winning adds to the fun, and lessons help you win, so chess lessons should be fun. A good guideline is "If you are not having fun, you are in the wrong place!" – and most professional instructors do their best to ensure that lessons are fun for each and every student. It is a job for them, but a game to their students and their parents.

However, not everything is always ideal. Most students and parents pick general improvement as their goal; if so, you are paying your instructor to help your child get better and most instructors take that responsibility very seriously. If students want to improve as much as the best young

players do, then a *lot* of work is involved. All chess masters did that work, primarily because they thought it was fun – but not everyone feels this way.

Not everyone wants to pay the price to get better – and that is OK! Many students do NOT really want to get better if they actually have to work at it, or if they must *take time to think during every move of a game*. However, a good instructor should expect his students to try their best when playing.

There is no magic to getting better … So a basic dilemma exists: for those really expecting to improve, getting better requires effort. Beginners might be asked at least to play and record games and/or to do some tactical problems. While this work *would* be expected for music lessons, chess is a game, so sometimes parents and students don't expect that they must make that same effort. There is no fairy dust an instructor can sprinkle on the student to make him magically better!

Think out your goals carefully – maybe just playing in tournaments would be better …

Some young students who love to play chess, especially those below age 9, would be better off with just an occasional lesson, concentrating instead primarily on playing in tournaments, or at a club, until their desire to improve becomes great enough to motivate them to work. For most students, playing in tournaments is great fun. Of course, without work, many of chess' beneficial side effects – disciplined thinking, organizational skills, rewards from your efforts, etc. – are diminished, but sometimes it is better not to throw out the baby with the bathwater. Keep playing tournaments for fun!

If the work is fun, then the work will get done …

Students who enjoy the lessons the most are the ones with the most lofty goals and who enjoy the work. Not coincidentally, these are also the ones who reap the biggest benefits, in terms of self-esteem and satisfaction, not just winning. A good percentage of students do enjoy the work, but for some more moderate expectations are reasonable and maybe even more beneficial. The ideal is for chess to remain a fun game for all!

I once read that chess has more books written about it than all the other games put together (although this was before they wrote books about video-gaming strategy!). Opinions vary greatly about which books, videos, and software are best (see chapter 3). A lot depends upon the following factors:

❖ Is your child better at aural or visual input? If visual only, he may prefer books; if he listens better, then videotapes may be a better way to go. Most chess book sellers also stock videos. Today there are dozens of videos available for all levels of play.

❖ Age of the reader. Some children are so young that the parents need an adult-level beginners book, so that they can transfer the information to the child. Older children can read for themselves with books targeted for the 8-10 year old range.

❖ How advanced is the player? Some players are way beyond pure beginner books, while many others could certainly benefit from reading some good elementary texts!

For beginner chess books, here are some of my recommendations:

❖ *The Complete Idiot's Guide to Chess* (2nd Edition), by Grandmaster Patrick Wolff – Don't let the title fool you! This is an excellent book for beginners over the age of 10 (youngsters would have to be helped by an older reader – it is not written at their level). It covers not only how to play, but many of the same tips I give my students. Good for students up to the 1000-1200 level!

❖ *Everyone's Second Chess Book*, by Dan Heisman – Board Vision, Tips, Etiquette, Rules, etc. This is the book that has all my recommendations for both beginning and intermediate adults, and younger students all rolled into one place!

❖ *Square One*, by Bruce Pandolfini – A detailed book teaching very young beginners how to play.

❖ *Pandolfini's Endgame Course*, by Bruce Pandolfini – straightforward examples of basic ideas for the final part of a game.

❖ *Comprehensive Chess Course, Vol II* , by GM Lev Alburt (Vol I primarily just teaches you how to play) – Youngsters can use this in conjunction with Bain's book (see next) for a real good start.

❖ *Chess Tactics for Students* (Student Edition), by John Bain – My first recommendation for learning tactical motifs (pins, forks, double attacks, discovered checks, back-rank mates, etc.)

❖ *The Chess Tactics Workbook*, by Al Wollum – Somewhat similar to Bain's book but with more problems overall and more mate problems, but less single-motif problems.

❖ *Logical Chess Move by Move*, by Irving Chernev – A classic which explains each move in delightful detail!

For more advanced students:

❖ *1,001 Winning Chess Sacrifices and Combinations*, by Fred Reinfeld – The best way for all players below "advanced" to improve is to do tactical problems. Once you learn the motifs, you learn about "combinations" of motifs, and this is a book with lots of them. Use after Bain's *Chess Tactics for Students*. This book uses the older descriptive notation.

❖ *Nunn's Chess Openings* (NCO) , by Nunn, Burgess, Emms & Gallagher – Every intermediate can use a one-volume encyclopedia covering all the openings. This 1999 book is up-to-date and edited by Dr. John Nunn, one of the best chess writers today (although this particular work has very little text). The updated *Modern Chess Openings* (14th edition, a.k.a. *MCO-14*) is also good.

❖ *Chess Endings: Essential Knowledge*, by GM Yuri Averbakh – This small book contains all the basics for chess endgames.

❖ *Chess Training Pocket Book*, by GM Lev Alburt – the 300 most instructive positions.

❖ *Most Instructive Games of Chess Ever Played*, by Irving Chernev – 62 annotated games, each with an in-structive theme – written at a good intermediate level.

❖ *Understanding Chess Move by Move*, by GM John Nunn – sort of a modern cross between Chernev's *Most Instructive Games of Chess Every Played* and *Logical Chess Move by Move* but more advanced than either. Another good one by Nunn.

❖ *The Amateur's Mind*, by IM Jeremy Silman – Great book that goes through many of the faulty thinking pro-cesses.

❖ *Pawn Power in Chess*, by Hans Kmoch (or, similarly, Andrew Soltis' *Pawn Structure Chess*) – a book about how to use pawns. Archaic nomenclature, but great ideas.

❖   *Elements of Positional Evaluation*, by Dan Heisman – explains some of the most basic ideas about how pieces get their value and power – written for those above age 12.

5.5 Top Tips for Young Players

Many books have tips, guidelines, or principles for beginning students. While these are not a primary purpose of this book, the author has extensive experience instructing young players, so I thought it would be nice to include some tips for parents to share with their kids:

1. <u>The most important chess guideline</u>: SAFETY = Keep all your pieces safe! (and consider taking opponent's pieces that are not safe). You must make all your decisions before you touch a piece. If you touch a piece and then see that something will not be safe, it is too late, because if you touch a piece you must move it.

2. <u>The 2nd most important chess guideline</u>: ACTIVITY = Make sure all your pieces are doing something all the time! – So, for example, move every piece once before you move any piece twice in the opening (as a goal). Often the best strategy in a position with no tactics is to take a piece that is not  doing much and find a move that helps it to do more!

3. You are trying to find the BEST move, so when you see a good move, look for a better one. If you don't look, you can't see!

4. After your opponent makes a move, ask yourself "Why

did he do that?" and "What can he do to me now that he couldn't do to me before?" See what has changed and how that affects everything. And check to see if that piece or any other opponent's piece is not safe.

5. TAKE YOUR TIME – if world championship players always take several minutes to find a good move, what makes you think that you can find a better one faster? Look at it this way: NOTHING is preventing you from playing like stronger players do, and taking your time to look at as many possibilities as you can.

6. The way to keep your pieces safe and to win your opponent's pieces is through tactics, the science of chess safety. Tactics are the most important part of a chess game – <u>every</u> good player knows basic tactics cold. The most basic tactic is *counting* – that is, making sure each piece is adequately guarded enough times by other pieces. Studying the other tactics: Pins, forks, check-mates, skewers, removal of the guard,  queening combinations, double threats, discovered checks, etc. can be done first through a book like Bain's *Tactics for Students* or Wollum's *The Chess Tactics Workbook*, and then Reinfeld's *1,001 Sacrifices and Combinations*. If you like doing the puzzles in those books, you will probably do all of them and become a good player! By the way, the player who gets the most pieces out first usually finds himself on the good side of the tactics!

7. For piece values, start with pawn = 1 pawn; bishop and knight = 3 pawns; rook = 5 pawns; and queen = 9 pawns. More advanced players should think of bishops and knights as worth about 3¼ pawns, a queen about 9¾. Having two bishops when your opponent does not is called "the bishop pair" and is worth about an extra ½ pawn. Winning a rook

for a bishop or knight is called winning *the Exchange* and is worth a little more than half a piece (bishop or knight).

8. When you are considering which move to make, consider first your checks, captures, and threats – similarly, when trying to see what your opponent can do to you, look for *his* checks, captures, and threats first.

9. Your opponent is just as important as you are. Make sure you pay just as much attention to what he is doing as to what you are doing.

10. Eliminate fuzzy thinking – everything on the board is visible. Something is either a threat or it is not – you have to do the work to figure it out. Don't fall for lazy thinking like, "I *think* his piece might get into danger"; either it will be in trouble or it won't, and if you can figure it out in your available time, you should!

11. Three things you should try to do in the *opening*:

   A. Get ALL your pieces into play ("development")
   B. Get some control of the center
   C. Castle your king into safety

12. Other opening guidelines: Move knights before bishops – as a general move order, move out the knight on the side where you want to castle, then the bishop, then castle, then move your other knight, your other bishop, move the queen up a little and then move both rooks where they will do some good. Don't start an attack until ALL your pieces are ready. Don't move up your queen too far where your opponent's knights and bishops can attack her and win

tempi (time). The player who makes the *best* use of his rooks (and the *fastest* use) usually wins the opening!

13. A few good endgame tips are: 1) The king is a strong piece – make sure you use it. 2) Rooks belong behind passed pawns, 3) Passed pawns usually should be pushed.

14. Many things in chess are easy! Taking your time to look for more reasonable moves - and what your opponent can do IF you make them - is a habit that all good players have, and you can, too, if you just try on each and every move, without fail!

15. A good attitude is important. No matter how strong my opponent is, I *never* think, "I am going to lose this game" before it even starts! I just feel like I have to take my time and play my best no matter whom I am playing. If I win, fine; if I lose, then I want to learn why I lost so I won't ever lose that way again!

More helpful beginner tips can be found at www.uschess.org/beginners/ and other instructional websites.

Chapter 6

The Personal Side of Chess

6.1 Chess, Kids, and Competition

This is a tricky subject. There are two extreme views:

John Wayne: "Competition is good for kids – they may as well get used to it. The sooner they learn to play and win the sooner they will be ready for real life."

Alan Alda: "Games are for fun and it shouldn't matter whether you win or lose. Once you start keeping score, then the pressure to win negatively affects both the competitors and their parents. This pressure and the feeling that 'if you don't win it is bad' is not good for young kids, and maybe not even good for them as they get older."

Luckily for parents of both views, chess can be taken either way, and for most of us the truth lies somewhere in between.

Sure, chess has rules that say when the game is a win, loss, or draw, and of course the object is to do the best you can, and winning is considered "better" than drawing or losing.

But "doing the best you can" can also mean learning to take your time and play the best you can, no matter what the result. My students know that I always look at my watch when they have finished a game. If they played too fast, then they were not trying their best, and I don't really care whether they won or lost. When my students play hard and long, then I tell them I am proud of them no matter what the result. But for those John Waynes out there, I

111

might add that if you try your best you are much more likely to win, too!

One thing is certain: parents should teach their child as early as possible that losses are part of the chess experience and should be viewed as a learning experience. Any child who views a loss as something to be forgotten will never become a really good player.

Both extremes are bad: if someone does not mind losing at all, he will likely make the same mistake over and over; on the other hand, if losing is taken so personally that the loser gets upset and cannot learn from his losses, then that also is not good emotionally, nor conducive to learning.

A child should review the game later with a better player (ideally an instructor) to learn what he did wrong, so he can apply that lesson to later games. What really makes someone better is identifying one's mistakes and minimizing or eliminating them. Personally, I was very good at doing this for myself, and that is one reason why I think I became a good player quickly. The best players have lost more games than most people will ever dream of playing, so it is part of the game: losing should be a positive learning experience.

6.2 Making Friends

The world of chess is amazing. You meet many people from different areas of the country and even the world, with a variety of backgrounds and cultures, who all share the same hobby and speak a common cultural language. I could relate many stories of how my son or I were helped out by others whom we met through chess. So could most experienced tournament players. My son views tournaments as giant pizza and Chinese food parties where he meets with old friends from all over the East Coast. Whenever he goes to a tournament, one of the first topics is

"Who else is playing?". Now that my son is in college he knows players at dozens of other colleges who played with him during his scholastic tournament days.

So when you go to a tournament, it is both sociable and fun to get to know the other players. The skittles room is a great place to chat and find a friendly game. At first it may seem like everyone knows everyone else and you don't, but if you think about it, that is good! It means there is one big community which is open to all, and unless for some reason you don't wish to belong, you and your family will soon become a welcome part of it. So join the fun!

6.3 Handling Ups and Downs

The Swiss system generally helps a player "find his level" – the better players end up playing the better players and the weaker players the other weak ones. Nevertheless, it is obvious that the better players win more and the weakest players lose the most. However, everyone goes through periods when he is not playing his best, and often even mediocre players have great days – it is nice to be human.

But dealing with these slumps and streaks can sometimes be difficult. A slumping chess player, like a baseball hitter, can get depressed: he may want to quit the tournament, not act as a good sport, ignore advice which will eventually make him a better player, or even feel like giving up chess altogether. Different personalities need to be handled differently, but some general advice can help a "slumper" or someone coming off a tough loss:

❖   "It is only a game – what is important is that you learned something and you can apply it to do better next time."

❖ "Cheer up! Everyone has bad days and you are just getting yours out of your system."

❖ "Won't you feel good when you continue to study and next time you play these players you can show them how much you have improved?"

❖ "Next time just remember some of the most important principles, and if you apply them on every move you are sure to do better: take your time, think before you touch, make sure all your pieces are safe and active, and when you see a good move, look for a better one."

❖ "So you lost a chess game – if that is the worst thing that happens to you, you will be the happiest person on the planet! So relax, get something to eat, and go in there and try your best next time. We love you the same whether you win or lose."

❖ "In every game there is only one point to be shared among two players, so at least half the players end up not winning no matter how good they are. So long as you did the best you can, you can be proud of your result and in the long run you will get your share of those points."

A swelled head can sometimes be tougher to deal with than a depressed loser. Players who beat others consistently sometimes attach more than just chess prowess to their success. They might believe it is their natural superiority. Of course, Albert Einstein was not a very good chess player because he did not study chess, and outside of tournaments you can almost always hand-pick opponents who know less about chess than you do. If your child does get a swelled head, here are some possible remedies:

❖   Next time enter him in a tougher tournament or tougher section. The Lord of the Beginners might be the Doormat of the Intermediates.

❖   Remind him that chess is just a game, and that beating someone does not make him superior in any way, any more than a fast sprinter is "superior" to most runners in anything except foot speed.

❖   Tell him that no one likes someone with a swelled head, so he should keep things in perspective for other times when he's not doing so well, or when he has to deal with these same people away from a chess board!

❖   Tell him overconfident players do not always play their best, so if he wants to continue to do well, he had better avoid feeling he can win by doing whatever he wants.

❖   Sneak in a much higher-rated player (a "ringer") against him in a fun game. Getting soundly beaten sometimes works wonders to restore perspective, especially if the high-rated player remains anonymous. This may seem drastic, but when all else fails, it sometimes works!

6.4 Dealing with Opponents (and spectators who seem like opponents)

Everyone has to interact with his opponents, especially if the opponents are human, and not a computer at home (some people prefer the computers for that reason!). Most opponents are very nice and conscious of chess etiquette, but in scholastic tournaments this percentage may be lower than we would all wish.

First, how someone should deal with a normal opponent:

❖   Shake hands before and after the game.

❖   Before the game a little chat is OK.

❖   Do not say anything during the game except game-oriented comments like, "Would you like a draw?" or "Touch move" or "I resign." Chatting during the game is not only forbidden, but also bothers those playing around you.

❖   If your opponent insists on talking or is doing anything non-malicious to disturb you and will not stop upon polite request, stop your clock and get the TD.

❖   After the game, wait until the set owner puts the set away. Then both players should mark the results on the pairing sheet. After that, if you have time, sometimes it is fun to go over the game in the skittles room.

❖   Do not stop the clock unless you either 1) have finished the game, 2) have messed up the board and need to have the TD help you reset it, or 3) have a claim or question for the tournament director. The clock cannot be stopped for recording moves, going to the bathroom, etc.

❖   If anything strange, or which you don't know how to handle, is going on, stop the clock and get the TD. This includes illegal positions, questions, claims, strange moves, whatever!

Dealing with a difficult opponent:

❖   First, it is NOT up to the player to deal with a difficult opponent. If ignoring an opponent is not possible, then a player should get the TD. The correct way to do this is to get the TD while your opponent is thinking or, if it is your turn, stop the clock and get the TD. Some scholastic TDs prefer that you just raise your hand, so if the TD has announced this policy, a player should raise his hand and wait instead of getting up.

❖   NEVER have an argument with an opponent. Once you do not agree on something, quickly stop the clock and get the TD. For example, if you say "That move is illegal" and your opponent says it is not, do not discuss it! Stop the clock, get the TD, and let him decide.

❖   If a person is bothering you in any way, there is a rule against that! Of course, he is allowed to do normal things, like breathe quietly. If *that* bothers you, then too bad. But if he is making noises or kicking you or shaking the table or blocking your view or saying things, get the TD and tell him what he is doing. You can try to deal with it quickly and quietly first, but if it fails (and it probably will fail if your opponent is doing it on purpose), then let the tournament director handle it. The TD can take a variety of steps to ensure that your opponent will stop.

In the long run, it is very difficult for someone deliberately to disturb your child, so long as you have taught him to get the TD. Since all the relevant rules require quiet with no disturbances of any kind, these rules can usually be used to support your child's wish to play without disturbance. Remember, the TD may have a lot of power, but he is not everywhere nor is he a mind-reader. Remember that parents must not interfere with a game in any way, including notifying the TD if there is a "game" problem (if a fight breaks out, interference is OK!). Interfering in any way affects the game and is not allowed. Therefore, you should train your child to get him and let him know what the problem is. Occasionally in a big tournament an assistant TD will not give you the proper help or satisfaction, sometimes just because he is not as familiar with the rules or does not have the authority to put a strong penalty on a player. In that case, you can always have your child request to talk to the senior TD in charge of the tournament.

It is important to teach your child not to believe his opponent when the subject is chess rules. Often older kids will tell younger kids all kinds of things that are just for the older kid's advantage, especially if they feel that is the only way to get a draw – or a win. Of course, almost none of these kids understand the rules any better than yours, so your child should not be intimidated, but learn to rely on what he already knows and especially what the TD tells him.

Dealing with Spectators

Many scholastic tournaments do not allow spectators. If you have seen *Searching for Bobby Fischer*, then you know why spectators – especially parents! – can strongly affect young players.

Secondly, tournament rules state that spectators basically have no rights, compared to a player. If a player complains that a spectator is bothering him, it really does not matter if that is true or not – the TD should tell the spectator to keep a distance from that board or politely ask him to leave the room. So if your child is bothered by a spectator, he should certainly not be intimidated – even if it is an adult – but instead promptly alert the TD. Spectator rules are listed in Appendix B.

6.5 Exceptional Children

It may not be surprising that a high percentage of parents whose children play chess consider them "exceptional children" – and many of them are! While chess is a great game for everyone and its benefits extend to all, there is no doubt that an extremely bright, competitive child might find chess his ideal sport, since he does not have to be as big and strong as a football star, nor as tall as many basketball players.

Almost all the advice in this book applies to exceptional children as well as normal ones. The exceptional child might start lessons or tournaments at an earlier age, but on the other hand his temperament, not his mental ability, may prevent him from doing so. A child with exceptional chess ability might not have exceptional maturity, so that "rushing" his development may be detrimental.

Having stated all that, here are some things that can be done with a chess "prodigy":

❖   Find him the best coach you can afford – don't switch coaches back and forth unless you are convinced your original choice was incorrect. Once someone finds you have a talented player, you may be tempted with many offers to help, but too many cooks may spoil the broth.

❖   Have him join a club and play slow chess regularly against players about 200 points stronger than he is. Ask the better players in the club to go over his games with him after he finishes, if they are willing. Playing extra games on an Internet server is also helpful so long as he does not develop bad habits by playing too many "blitz" games.It is also necessary for your child occasionally to play opponents rated 100-200 points lower, so he will learn how to win against resistant, but weaker competition.

❖   Play as many strong tournaments as possible. Play "up" (against stronger competition) as much as possible, but also occasionally let him play at his own level (especially in championships) to learn how to compete as a favorite against weaker players and how to play for possible prizes and titles. It is especially helpful in games like this for a young player to go to the skittles room after the game and analyze the moves with his stronger opponent, almost like a free lesson!

❖ Make sure he doesn't worry about his rating – tell him to play as much as possible and learn and enjoy himself! If he does, the rating gains will come naturally and with less stress.

❖ Consider attending a chess camp or two in the summer.

Summary for All Parents

The world of chess can be a wonderful place for parents and their children. It offers a great opportunity to expand your mind and develop social and mental skills. I hope the information in this book will help you and your child get started on this fascinating path and continue on it successfully.

This section is not an attempt to define the entire special vocabulary of chess, but it does include most terms a new player is likely to encounter in his early exploration of the game. Some terms here have been officially established for centuries, others are modern slang. Words in **boldface** in a definition have their own definitions elsewhere.

Action Chess: A game in which each player has 30 minutes to make all his moves.

Adjust: To center a **piece** in its square. If a player does not intend to move the adjusted piece, he must first say "I adjust" or "J' adoube," otherwise he can be required to move it by the **touch-move rule**. Adjusting should be done only on one's own time, and should not be done unnecessarily or too frequently, or it may be considered an attempt to annoy the opponent. Neither should a player purposely set his pieces badly off-center so that they require frequent adjusting.

Algebraic Notation: A method for recording moves, in which the **ranks** are numbered 1-8 and **files** are labeled a-h, starting at White's lower left corner, as shown in the **diagram**.

In this **position**, White's last move was 2. Bc4, or in long form, 2. Bf1-c4, meaning the bishop moved from the square f1 to c4. Originated in 19th-century Europe. Now used throughout most of the world, replacing the older descriptive notation in the USA circa 1970.

Amateur: In chess, this generally denotes a non-master, i.e. a person rated under 2200. At the US Amateur, masters cannot play. At the US Amateur Team tournaments, the average team **rating** must be below 2200. Note: in chess, amateurs can win money, sometimes quite a bit at the World Open and other large tournaments.

Analysis: A major part of the process of thinking about a chess **position**. It can involve both a general evaluation of the position, and a detailed examination of specific moves that can or should be played at a given point.

Annotation: Written **analysis**, usually in a book. A good annotator explains the reasons behind moves, points out errors and finds improvements for both players. Much of chess literature consists of annotated games.

Attack: This can have several meanings. Probably the two most common are: (1) To make a move that threatens to capture an undefended or under-defended **piece**. (2) A coordinated series of moves aimed at a target in the opponent's **position**, especially when the goal is to **checkmate** the king.

Back Rank: For White, the squares a1 to h1 are his "back rank"; for Black, the squares a8 to h8.

Back-Rank Mate: A **checkmate** on the 1st or 8th rank with a rook or queen. In this position

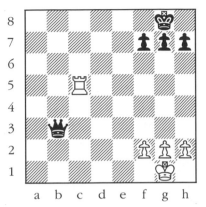

White to move could mate immediately with 1.Rc8, while Black to move could do so by 1...Qd1. Beginners are particularly prone to overlooking this kind of mate.

Blindfold play: To play without sight of the board, envisioning the position in one's mind. Difficult or impossible for most players, but some masters have excelled at it, playing several dozen such games simultaneously. The "blindfold" player's eyes are not actually covered; he simply is situated where he cannot see any board(s), and the moves arc conveyed to him verbally.

Blitz: Fast chess. Blitz games are often played at five minutes per player per game.

Blunder: A bad move, primarily one that turns a win into a loss or draw, or a draw into a loss. In **annotation**s a blunder is usually indicated by "??".

Book: In chess jargon, this usually refers to tried-and-true, well-analyzed opening lines that have been played for decades and published in chess books. Thus "book moves" and "book lines" are usually sound and can generally be played without further thought (though not always!). A player who has studied many openings in detail is said to be "well-booked." Also certain well-analyzed **endgame**s may be known as "book wins" or "book draws."

Brilliancy: A series of moves, usually involving a **sacrifice**, which shows impressive creativity, originality, artistry, and powers of **calculation**. An especially beautiful kind of **combination**. Some tournaments award "brilliancy prizes," and games containing great brilliancies are considered "immortal games." In **annotation**s, a brilliant move is usually indicated by "!!".

Bughouse: A variant of chess with two-man teams playing against each other on two separate boards. Pieces captured by a player on one board can be used by his teammate on the other board. Very popular among scholastic players.

Bye: Special provision for a player who can't or won't play a round at some point in a tournament, but who still wants to continue in the tournament. See Chapter 4 for a full explanation.

Calculation: The specific kind of **analysis**: detailed examination of possible moves and their consequences. Commonly called "seeing ahead." A learned skill that can be developed by practice and study of **tactics**.

Capture (or Take): To remove a piece from the board by a legal move. *Not* to be called "kill" or "jump." In a **game score**, captures are usually indicated by "x", e.g. Bxg7 would mean a bishop captured something on g7.

Castle: "Castling" is a special move designed to protect the king. The king is moved two squares toward an unmoved rook, and the rook moved to the other side of the King. This is *not* another term for a rook, though that is a common mistake.

Center: Usually defined as the four innermost squares of the board: d4, e4, d5, and e5 (marked "+" in the diagram). Some authorities include the squares d3, e3, c4, c5, f4, f5, d6 and e6 (marked "x" in the diagram).

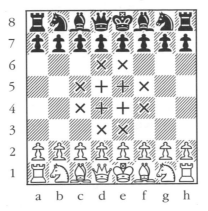

Control of the center is very important in chess, especially in the **opening** and **middlegame**. A player who controls most of the central squares usually has a big advantage.

CFC: Chess Federation of Canada.

Cheapo: Slang term for a **trap**, especially a superficial one.

Check: A move which attacks the opposing king. A king so attacked is said to be "in check." You do *not* have to announce "check" out loud. In a **game score**, check is usually indicated by "+".

Checkmate: A position in which a king is in **check**, and no legal move can get him out of check. Checkmate is the final goal in chess, and ends the game. Often called simply "mate." From the Persian *shah mat*, meaning "The king is dead." In a **game score**, mate is usually indicated by "#".

Chopping Wood: Slang term for **simplification**.

Clock: A chess timer, with two faces. Each face shows the thinking time of one player. When a player moves, he hits a button on his side of the clock, thus stopping his clock and starting his opponent's. Clocks can be analog (face and hands) or digital. If a player runs out of time before making the prescribed number of moves, and his opponent points this out, he loses if his opponent still has **mating material** on the board.

Coffee-house: A slang term covering a variety of chess styles and behaviors, all somewhat suspect or second-rate. "Coffee-house moves" are superficially impressive but unsound. "Coffee-house openings" are generally unorthodox. "Coffee-housing" means to feign exaggerated reactions to moves on the board, trying to distract or deceive the opponent (not permitted in serious games). A reference to chess in 18th- and 19th-century Europe, when it was often played in coffee houses and taverns.

Combination: A series of forcing moves, usually involving a **sacrifice**, to achieve a certain goal, often the win of **material** or **checkmate** of the opposing king, and usually combining two or more tactical motifs (hence the name "combination").

Correspondence chess: Chess played by opponents at a distance from each other, and involving long periods (sometimes days or weeks) between moves. Played by letter and postcard, and now increasingly by fax or e-mail. Some different rules apply than in **over-the-board chess**, for example players are allowed to consult books.

Counterplay: A player under **attack** may seek only to defend his own **position**, or he may be able also (or instead) to attack the opponent's position. In the latter case he is said to "have counterplay."

Counting: A method of determining whether a piece is safe on a square on which a series of **captures** is possible. If the number of defenders equals or exceeds the number of attackers, the piece is usually adequately defended. For example, in this diagram

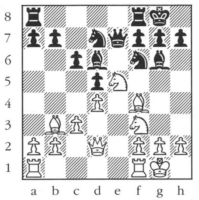

the knight on e5 is attacked by three black pieces (the queen on e7, the bishop on d6, and the knight on d7), but it is also defended by three (the knight on f3, the bishop on f4, and the pawn on d4). Therefore it is adequately defended for the moment.

Defense: (1) A move or moves intended to counter a **threat**. (2) An **opening** by Black, chosen to counter a particular opening by White, e.g. the Sicilian Defense, the King's Indian Defense, etc.

Development: The process of getting one's pieces into active play, usually in the **opening** phase of the game. The player who gets his pieces off the **back rank** and developed to active posts sooner usually has an advantage.

Diagonal: A row of connected squares at a 45-degree angle to a **rank** or **file**. Diagonals are usually named for their starting and ending squares; for example the x-marked squares here

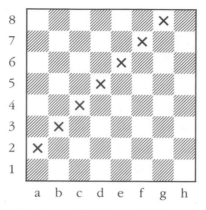

are the "a2-g8 diagonal." The a1-h8 and a8-h1 lines are called the "long diagonals."

Diagram: A pictorial representation of a chess **position**.

Discovery: An **attack** by a **line piece** occurring when a pawn or **piece** moves out of its way. If the piece thus attacked is a king, it is called "discovered check." In this position,

any move by the bishop on g2 creates a discovered check on the black king.

Double Attack: A single move that carries out an attack on two (or more) pieces. In the above diagram, the move Bd5+ would attack both Black's king and queen, allowing White to play Bxc4 next move.

Doubled Pawns: Two pawns of the same color on the same **file**, resulting from a **capture**.

Doubled Rooks: Two rooks standing on the same **file**, or less often, the same **rank**, with no obstruction between them.

Draw: Any game that ends in neither player winning, by **stalemate**, lack of **mating material**, 50-Move Rule, three-fold repetition, mutual agreement, etc. A draw scores ½-point for both players.

Elo: The **rating** system used by the **USCF** and **FIDE** was devised by Dr. Arpad Elo, a mathematician. Therefore a player's rating is sometimes called his "Elo rating" or simply his "Elo."

Endgame: The last stage of a chess game, after the **opening** and **middlegame**, when **material** is greatly reduced and the kings can safely become active. Pawn **promotion** is often a major goal in the endgame.

En Passant: French for "in passing." When a pawn on its original square advances two squares, an adjacent enemy pawn on the same rank may capture it as if it moved only one square, but *on the next move only*. For example, if in this position

Black were to play d7-d5, White could, on his next move only, play e5xd6, capturing the pawn as if it had moved only one square. Pronounced "on pah-SOHNT."

En prise: From French, referring to an undefended (or under-defended) piece (other than the king) that is vulnerable to **capture**. "You were doing fine until you put that rook *en prise*." Pronounced "on preez."

Exchange: A series of **capture**s, at the end of which neither side has gained material. For example, if White moves his queen to capture Black's queen, then Black captures White's queen with another piece, they are said to "exchange queens."

Exchange, the: To "win the Exchange" means to **capture** a rook, while losing a **minor piece**. To give up a rook intentionally for a minor piece is to "**sacrifice** the Exchange." Synonyms include "trade" and "swap."

Expert: A player with a **USCF rating** between 2000 and 2199.

Fianchetto: An Italian word, meaning to develop a bishop on one of the two long **diagonal**s, at b2 or g2 for White, or b7 or g7 for Black. Pronounced "fee-ahn-KET-toe."

FIDE: Acronym for the Fédération Internationale des Échecs, or International Chess Federation. Pronounced "fee-day."

FIDE Master (FM): The lowest international chess title bestowed by **FIDE**.

File: Any of the vertical rows of a chessboard. Usually called by their letter designation, e.g. the squares e1 to e8 are called "the e-file." Also sometimes named for the piece occupying that file in the opening array, i.e. "king file" instead of e-file.

Five-Minute: A game where each player has five minutes to make all his moves.

Flag: The part of an analog clock that rises when the minute hand nears the hour and falls at the hour. "His flag fell" means a player ran out of time.

Flanks: The two areas of the chessboard other than the d- and e-files, i.e. the rectangles with corners at a1/a8/c8/c1 (sometimes called "the queen's flank") and f1/f8/h8/h1 (sometimes called "the king's flank"). An **opening** involving play in these areas, and which delays advance of the d- and e-pawns, is sometimes called a "flank opening." An advance in one of these areas is sometimes called a "flank **attack**."

Fool's Mate: The shortest possible game, one sample being 1.f3? e5 2.g4?? Qh4#.

Forfeit: (1) A game lost because a player failed to show up, or (2) a game lost by exceeding the time limit.

Fork: A **double attack** by a single **man**, usually a **knight** or pawn. In the diagrammed position,

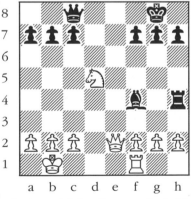

White has two forks at his disposal: 1 Ne7+, forking king and queen, or g2-g3, forking bishop and rook.

Gambit: An **opening** involving an early offer of **material**, usually a pawn, sometimes two, more rarely a **minor piece**. For example 1 e4 e5 2 f4 is called the King's Gambit. From the Italian *gambetta*, a wrestling maneuver that trips the opponent.

Game score: The record of the moves of a game. Not to be confused with a player's score, i.e. his won/lost/drawn record in a **match** or tournament.

Grandmaster: (GM): The highest international chess title awarded by **FIDE**.

Hang a piece: Slang for putting a piece **en prise** and losing it, or for overlooking a simple combination that loses a piece. "He was playing well, but then he hung his queen."

Heavy piece: see **major piece**.

Illegal Move: One that either (a) moves a **piece** in an illegal manner, e.g. moving a bishop like a rook, or (b) results in an illegal position, such as putting one's king in **check**.

International Master: (IM): The intermediate international chess title, above FM but below GM.

Isolated Pawn: A pawn with no other pawns of the same color on adjacent **file**s.

Kibitzer: A German word, meaning a spectator who offers unasked-for advice about a game in progress. Sometimes acceptable in a **skittles** game, *never* in a serious game.

Kingside: The half of the board on which the kings stand in the opening array, i.e. the rectangle with corners at e1, e8, h8 and h1.

Knight: *Not* to be called a "horse," though in most sets it looks like one. It begins the game between the bishop and rook and moves like an "L".

Line piece: A rook, bishop, or queen. So called because they always move in straight lines.

Major piece: A rook or queen. So called because they are generally stronger than the **minor pieces**.

Man: Any chess piece, including pawns.

Master: A player with a **USCF rating** between 2200 and 2399. Also called "National Master" or NM.

Match: A series of games between two players only, as opposed to a tournament, which involves three or more playing each other. A "team match" is actually a set of individual games.

Material: The men on the board at any point in a game, excluding kings. To have a "material advantage" is to have **piece**s of a greater total value, usually figured by the formula: pawn = 1, bishop or **knight** = 3, rook = 5, queen = 9. This formula does not apply in all **position**s, however, and should be used only as a rough guide.

Mating material: With all other **men** except kings off the board, forcing **checkmate** requires that one player have at least a queen, or a rook, or two bishops (moving on different-colored squares), or bishop and **knight**, or at least one pawn (which may be promoted to rook or queen). If neither player has this (e.g. one has only a bishop, the other only a knight), the game is drawn. If a player runs out of time, but his opponent does not have mating material, the game is drawn.

Middlegame: The phase of the game following the **opening** and preceding the **endgame**. Very hard to define precisely, but usually, roughly, beginning around move 10 or 20, when most or all **piece**s have been developed, and ending around move 40 or whenever **material** is reduced to the endgame stage. Usually the most complex phase of a game.

Minor piece: A **knight** or bishop.

Odds: Any method of compensating for different skill levels between opponents. Decades ago material odds were commonly given; the stronger player might start without one of his pawns, knights, or rooks. More common today are time odds, where the weaker player is given more time than the stronger, e.g. 10 minutes to 5.

Open File: A file containing no pawns of either side.

Opening: The first phase of a game, roughly the first 10 or 20 moves. **Development** and control of the **center** are important goals in the opening. Over the years a multitude of standard openings have been devised, named and analyzed to a high degree, some of the most popular being the Ruy Lopez, the French Defense, the Queen's Gambit, etc. Study of openings becomes more important after one has learned chess fundamentals.

Over-the-board chess: Chess played face-to-face, as opposed to **correspondence chess**. Abbreviated "OTB chess."

Pairing: A specific set of opponents for a **round**. A pairing list tells the players who has White or Black, and which board number each is to play on.

Passed pawn: A pawn which has no enemy pawns in

front of it on the same or adjacent **file**s. How far the pawn has advanced is irrelevant. In this position,

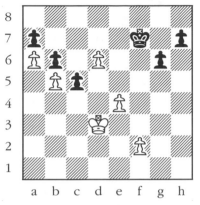

White has passed pawns at d6 and e4, Black has passed pawns at c5 and h7. Passed pawns become especially important in the **endgame** due to the threat of **promotion**. Two passed pawns of the same color on adjacent files are called "connected passed pawns" (e.g. White's d- and e-pawns here).

Patzer: Slang for a weak player. Other similar terms include fish, woodpusher, and woodshifter.

Perpetual check: A situation in which a player cannot or does not force **checkmate**, but can give an endless series of **check**s. Usually done to force a **draw** bythree-fold repetition of a position.

Piece: (1) Any of the chess men, as in "Get all the pieces out of the bag." (2) A non-pawn, as in "You have to develop all your pieces." (3) A bishop or knight, as in "That wins a piece." or "I am up a piece."

Pin: A situation in which a **line-piece** holds down an enemy **man** due to the fact that a more valuable piece lies beyond it. In this position,

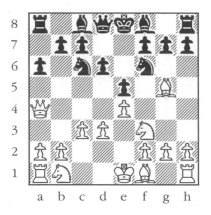

Black's **knight** at f6 is pinned by the bishop on g5, since any move by the knight would allow capture of the queen. Black's knight on c6 is also pinned, since to move it would expose the king to **check** (this is called an "absolute pin"). A move such as Be7 or b7-b5 would be said to "break the pin."

Ply: A half-move, or the move of one player. When both players move, that is two ply, or one full move. To calculate "I take, then he takes, then I take," is to look 3 ply ahead.

Position: The placement of men on the board at any given point in the game. Various terms are used to describe different kinds of positions: "free" or "cramped"; "open" or "closed"; "simple" or "complicated"; "developed" or "undeveloped" etc. "Positional judgement," the ability to evaluate the strengths and weaknesses of a position, is a skill good players develop.

Post-mortem: Slang term for a discussion of a game after it is over, trying to determine critical mistakes and better moves that might have been played. Young players should always do this whenever possible, especially when the opponent is a stronger player, as they can often learn from it.

Promotion: When a pawn is moved to the last **rank**, it cannot remain a pawn, but *must* be promoted to a piece other than a king. Promotions are usually to a queen, but a rook, bishop, or knight can be chosen (this is called "under-promotion"). Note: the promotion does *not* have to be to a piece already removed from the board by **capture**. Thus one may have two or more queens (or three rooks, etc.) on the board at once.

Queenside: The half of the board on which the queens stand in the opening array, i.e. the rectangle with corners at a1, a8, d8 and d1.

Rank: Any of the horizontal rows of squares on the chessboard. In **algebraic notation** the ranks are numbered 1 through 8 starting from White's side of the board. However, in a holdover from descriptive notation, the 2nd rank is sometimes called "Black's 7th rank."

Rating: A mathematical measure of chess performance. The **USCF** and **FIDE** use the **Elo** Rating System. Theoretically ratings start at 0 (basically impossible to get this low – no one ever has) and range upward indefinitely, but the highest ratings achieved so far (by such players as Bobby Fischer and Garry Kasparov) are around 2800. Most scholastic beginners start around 500; the average American adult rating is around 1500. Most grandmasters are in the 2500-2650 range.

Recapture: To **capture** a piece which had just captured another.

Resign: To concede defeat in a game, without playing on to **checkmate**. Usually done when a player considers his **position** hopeless. One resigns by purposely laying down one's king, or saying "I resign." Note that shaking hands or stopping the **clock** does not end a game.

Round: A set of games in a tournament, normally beginning all at the same time, with **pairing**s made by the **TD**.

Round Robin: A tournament in which each player eventually plays every other player; also called "all-play-all." Common in professional chess, but rare in scholastic chess. Unlike a **Swiss system** tournament, it calls for a commitment by the players to complete all their games.

Sacrifice: A move in which one player deliberately gives up a **man** of higher value for one of lower value, or gives up a man for nothing, in order to gain a more important goal. For example, in this position

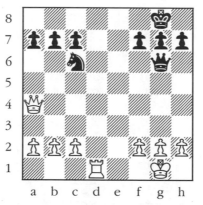

White has two winning sacrifices: either 1.Qxc6!, since no matter how Black **recaptures**, White can force a **back-rank mate** by 2.Rd8 next move; or even better, White can play 1.Rd8+!, forcing 1...Nxd8, after which White mates by 2.Qe1#.

Scholar's Mate: To mate on f7 (or, for Black, f2) with a queen and bishop in 4 moves (see chapter 4 for an example). Usually a very bad thing to try for. When teaching Scholar's Mate, I call it "Dumb and Dumber."

Scoresheet: A paper on which the moves of a game are recorded.

Section: A designated group of players in a chess tournament. In a multi-section tournament players in a given section are usually paired only with each other. Sections may be classified by rating, age, grade, scholastic/non-scholastic, etc.

Semi-Open File: A **file** containing pawns of only one color – it is "semi-open" for the other player.

Senior Master: A player with a **USCF rating** over 2399.

Simplification: The process of lessening the **material** on the board by **exchange**s. Usually advantageous for a player with a material advantage. For example, if one is a pawn ahead, it is often wise to simplify down to a **position** with only kings and pawns, to make it easier to promote the extra pawn.

Shot: Slang term for a strong move that catches the opponent by surprise.

Simul: Slang for "simultaneous exhibition," a special chess event in which a player, usually one of master strength or better, plays several different opponents "simultaneously," walking from board to board, moving quickly. Some GMs have played simuls vs. hundreds of opponents, usually winning about 90% of the games. Usually very interesting to watch, and very instructive for the participants.

Skewer: The reverse of a **pin**. A **tactic** in which a **line-piece** attacks an enemy **man**, which is forced to move and expose a man beyond it to **capture**. In this position, White to move could play 1 Rd1+ and 2 Rxd8, winning Black's queen by skewer, or Black to move could play 1...Bg7+ and 2...Bxa1, skewering the white queen. Also called "X-ray attack."

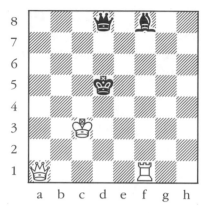

Skittles: Chess for fun or chess without a clock. A *skittles room* is where you go and play for fun while waiting for your next formal pairing.

Space: In chess, to have a "space advantage" means to control more of the board than the opponent. Often the player with more space has the more mobile pieces and is better able to create or defend against **threat**s.

Stalemate: A **position** in which a player has no legal move, but is not in check. By rule the game is a **draw**. For example in this position,

if it is Black's move he is stalemated: his pawn is blocked, and any move by king or knight puts him in **check**. This is a rule commonly misunderstood by young players, who sometimes let games they could win become draws by allowing stalemate.

Strategy: (1) The more general kind of **analysis**: the process of deciding on long-term objectives and devising plans to achieve them; (2) any of several standard plans known to be useful in a given **position**, e.g. "a strategy of rapid **development**," or of "gaining **space**," or of "**simplification**." Strategy involves setting goals; **tactics** are the means by which the goals are carried out.

Sudden Death: A time control period in which all remaining moves must be played within a certain amount of time on a player's clock. For example, "G/30" means a player has 30 minutes for the whole game; "40/1, SD/30" means he must make his first 40 moves before his clock advances one hour, and if the game continues beyond move 40, another 30 minutes is added to his clock for the rest of the game.

Swindle: A situation in which a player is theoretically lost, but by clever resistance, and mistakes by his opponent, he manages to draw or win.

Swiss System: A method for tournament pairings. Players are paired according to their scores and ratings, usually against others who are doing about equally well. Whenever possible, a player gets an equal number of games as Black and White (or as near equal as possible in an odd number of rounds), and does not play the same opponent twice. See Chapter 4 for details.

Tactics: The aspect of chess that involves **threat**s and prevention of threats. For example after 1 e4 e5 2 Nf3, White threatens to take Black's e-pawn; if Black replies 2...Nc6 that threat is prevented by the knight's defending the pawn. Where **strategy** involves general plans, tactics involve specific **calculation**. If strategies are the ends, tactics are the means. There are many tactical motifs: **pin**s, **fork**s, **double attack**s, **skewer**s, and countless others. Improvement in chess requires learning as many of these as possible.

TD: Tournament Director

Team Tournament: An event in which teams of players are matched against other teams. Individual pairings are usually in rating order, i.e. the highest-rated player on Team A plays against the highest-rated of Team B on Board 1, the second-highest play on Board 2, etc. Standings are based primarily on team-match results, not individual points. For example, in a 5-round tournament of 4-man teams, a team that won 5 matches, all by 2½-1½ scores, places higher than one that won 4 matches by 4-0 scores and drew one match 2-2.

Tempo: A move by one player, i.e. a **ply** or "half-move." The gain or loss of one or more tempi can be important. To "gain a tempo" means to reach a **position** in N moves that otherwise would require N+1 moves; to "lose a tempo" is do in N+1 moves what otherwise could be done in N moves. Tempi are often gained by **threat**s, for example, after 1 e4 d5 2 exd5 Qxd5 3 Nc3 Qd8, White has gained a tempo due to the threat to Black's queen. New players are sometimes confused when they read about "an advantage in time"; this usually does not refer to clock time, but means that one player has gained several tempi at his opponent's expense. An advantage of three tempi is generally considered equivalent to being a pawn ahead.

Threat: A move which can win **material**, force **checkmate**, gain **tempi**, gain **space**, or obtain some sort of advantage if the opponent does not counter it. Attacks on under-defended pieces are an example of a threat.

Time Control: The time limit(s) in effect for a given game, e.g. "40 moves in 2 hours" or "Game in 60."

Time Delay: A feature of many computerized digital clocks, whereby the clock does not start to run for a short interval (usually 2 to 30 seconds) after a player pushes his button; thus a player's clock will not advance if he consistently moves before the delay interval expires. Designed to avoid the mad sort of **time trouble** that can arise in **sudden death**.

Time trouble: A situation where a player must make too many moves in too little time, e.g. one minute for 20 moves. Increases the chance of **blunder**s. Some players are more prone to time trouble than others, and may lose games on the clock that could be won on the board. Young players must learn to avoid time trouble, but also must learn to take enough time to find good moves.

TL: Common abbreviation for "time limit" in tournament advertisements. The TLs in the entry on **time control** would be abbreviated 40/2 and G/60.

Trap: A deceptive move that seems to allow a strong reply, but prepares a stronger counter-blow in turn.

Touch-move rule: The rule that says: if you touch a piece you must move it; if you let go of a piece you have to leave it on that square; if you purposely displace an opponent's piece, you must take it. The only exceptions occur if a touched piece cannot be legally moved, a player has no legal move to a touched square, or no legal way to take a touched enemy piece. A very common misconception is

that a player may move a piece, then, if he did not fully release it, may return it to its original square and move another piece. In a serious game he would be required to move the piece he first touched, if it could be legally moved. If no legal move involving touched pieces can be made, no penalty is enforced.

Unrated: Someone who has never played a rated game, or whose rating has not yet been made official by the **USCF** (ratings become official every two months). An *unrated game* is one that is not played for a rating.

USCF: United States Chess Federation.

Wall Chart: Information posted during a tournament showing all players, usually in order of **section** and **rating**, with what color and result they had in each round. Results are shown cumulatively, so that a result line reading "1 1 2" means the player won in the first round, lost in the second (and thus still has 1), and won in the third.

Wing: Synonym for **flank**.

Zeitnot: German for **time trouble**. Pronounced "TSITE-note."

Zugzwang: German for "move compulsion"; a **position** in which any of a player's possible moves leads to a loss or disadvantage. Pronounced "TSOOG-tsvahng."

Zwischenzug: German for "in-between move." For example, giving **check** before an immediate **recapture**. Pronounced "TSVISH-en-tsoog."

APPENDIX B

A Guide for Spectator Conduct

(taken from the USCF National Scholastic Chess Tournament Regulations)

1. Do NOT stand in front of or make eye contact with the player whose game you are observing.

2. Do NOT "camp out" at one game.

3. Do NOT make faces or gestures or convey in any graphic way an opinion of a game being observed.

4. Do NOT discuss or even whisper opinions of a game being observed.

5. Do NOT speak privately with any player at or away from the board while his/her game is in progress.

6. Do NOT assume the role of TD and intervene for any reason such as pointing out illegal moves.

7. Do NOT make any noise, such as opening a bag of potato chips, within earshot of a game in progress.

8. Do NOT discuss a game at its conclusion if other games are being played in the vicinity, and do NOT analyze a game at a board in the tournament room.

9. Do NOT take pictures after the first ten minutes when using flash or a camera with an audible shutter.

10. Do NOT take pictures at any time from a location which makes you an obvious distraction to the players.

11. Do NOT attempt to enforce rules yourself.

12. DO report instances of cheating or rule violations by players or other spectators to the TD staff. Do NOT discuss instances of cheating or rules violations with the perpetrators.

13. DO comply with any requests or instructions issued by tournament staff.

Appendix C

Special Issues for Moms: "Chess Moms Speak"

By Lois Deckelbaum and Barbara Schoener

Our sons* entered the chess world with some naiveté. In an age where kids are struggling to find an identity through sport, academics, or social experiences, we, as parents, felt that chess was an acceptable forum into which to venture. The kids had a preconception that, in order to be a good player, they would only have to play a lot of games. What they were unprepared for was the amount of study, lessons, discipline and inevitable disappointment that is all part of "the game."

There are many things a child who is interested in playing chess can do. The basics are outlined in this and many other chess books. Basic openings must be learned, tactics explored, endgames mastered, and time-management understood. However, a more subtle and less defined area is the supportive role a parent can play in the game.

The role of a parent varies from child to child. Some children require a lot of attention while others shun the idea of having Mom around. The truth is that some tournaments are very time-consuming, expensive ventures. They can last 5 days. [*However many, if not most, scholastic tournaments last only one day, often from about morning until dinner. Championship events may be two or three days and important adult tournaments are almost always more than one day. – DH*] Registration, hotel, and food expenses can run to hundreds of dollars. The time spent can leave

*For somewhat unclear reasons, the vast majority of chess players are male. Although we use "he" in denoting the chess player, we encourage all girls/women to get involved in chess and enjoy!

147

the child emotionally and physically drained. Some careful planning and attention to the overall well-being of the child can make the experience considerably more enjoyable.

Among parents, the emotional and physical strain involved in chess is often underestimated. Although there is a difference between the needs of a four-year old child and those of a teenager, the basic concerns are the same. How the needs are met is the crucial difference. For example, all kids need to eat properly. Whether you come with food for a younger child or just make sure the older child has the money to buy food, the basic need must be addressed.

Sometimes decent food is scarce. Some parents pack a cooler. Depending on the tournament, it may be necessary to pack drinks, fruit and power bars. For longer tournaments, whole picnics can be taken (you'll get envious glances from the other families). Packing comfort foods for the tough or unexpected loss can help. It is important not to let your child's hunger level get too severe or else fatigue will set in. The result can be a less-than-optimum tournament outcome.

As you go to more and more tournaments, you will be surprised at the different conditions under which games are held. Some are in plush hotels with plenty of comfortable seating. Others are in back rooms of schools or churches. While the kids are fine, many times you will be relegated to the hard floor. Some people take lightweight beach chairs and leave them in their cars. In this way, your comfort is always assured.

It's to be hoped that your child will get proficient at using the time allotted for his game efficiently. If this is the happy case, you will need a distraction. You can almost lose your mind if you go empty-handed. Bringing needlepoint, magazines or newspapers works well. Because of potential interruptions, a thick novel can be hard to get into. It also limits you from networking with other families. You can make wonderful friends during the course of a game. These families can also be a great source of information about camps, clubs, and tournaments. For the younger player, using the restroom before the round starts can be a good idea. Many games have been lost due to a child rushing through moves due to "floating teeth." In longer games, it is possible to use a restroom while your opponent ponders his next move, but in a game with a time limit of 30 minutes per player, it can be detrimental to walk about.

In the event your child is done early, the time to the next game can stretch out boringly while his friends are still embroiled in their own games. A Gameboy, toys, or any enjoyable reading material will help pass the time. It will also provide an opportunity to share with other kids and pave the way to new friendships.

Alterations of sleep patterns can also be a concern. In some tournaments, games can go well past midnight. [Games in scholastic-only tournaments do not go late into the night, but if your child is playing in an adult tournament this is certainly possible. - DH] Controlling this variable is obviously difficult. I did take heed from one tournament when my son played to 1:30 AM. He eked out a victory in a tough match. However, even though he got to bed by 2:00, he was way off schedule. The next morning (even though play began at 12:00), he got uncharacteristically whipped. In this case, it would have been better to take the half-point bye and rest. By evening, he was feeling better but the whole tournament got off to a bad start and it was hard to recover.

When tournaments go for days (and even sometimes when they don't), it can be difficult for a parent to stay around.

Most people have complicated and hectic schedules. One possible solution is to share the "parenting." In other words, perhaps one mom or dad could be there from registration to lunch and another later on. This way, safety, food, and support issues can be easily addressed.

I believe it is up to each parent to determine if it is safe to leave his or her child. However, these are some of the variables you should consider. The age of the child is critical. It is not the tournament director's responsibility to assure the safety of your child. Accidents can happen when the time control is long and players finish early. Behavior must remain in accordance with tournament standards. Kids can venture outside. You must determine if the environment is safe, and determine what the consequences would be if your child did not listen and perhaps crossed the street to get food. Can he cross the street safely; can he pay attention to the time to make sure he is back in time to start his clock for the next round?

Registration is very often a confusing experience for first-time chess players. Often the fee is forgotten, USCF membership cards are misplaced, chess clocks broken, or chess pieces lost. Often, the child ends up rushing in at the last moment. All this can be very disconcerting for a child who is anxious about playing the game. These distractions can be almost overwhelming. Having a parent around who can find a solution is most reassuring.

One very important aspect of chess tournaments is the "social graces." These are basic rules of conduct applicable to any sport. It is always nice to have your child introduce himself and shake hands with his opponent prior to play. At the completion of the game, win or lose, he should know to shake hands again. If he lost, he is to congratulate his opponent graciously and say "good game" or something similarly appropriate. If he has been fortunate

 enough to win, he can try to find something positive to say about play during the game. Whether it is a compliment about a specific move or an invitation to go over the game in the skittles room, the good-natured gesture goes far to soften an otherwise painful defeat. Teaching your child to be a gracious and composed loser as well as a humble victor is a life-lesson that will serve him well in the future.

Having covered manners for children, it can be stated that adults also can display inappropriate behavior. There is always going to be the occasional "bad apple" wherever you go. To deal with this situation, you can go into the tournament room to help your child set up his board (though an older child will not like this idea and it is best to back off). Then, wish both players good luck and retreat to the back of the room or out of the room. However, some parents take another approach. They stay all the time. Some take a low profile being around only when needed. Some, however, hover around the chess board with their arms crossed in an authoritarian, supervisory manner. In the end, I am not sure if this benefits anyone. Both your child and his opponent can get very nervous. Is it really necessary to oversee the whole game? Would it not be just as appropriate to review the game after the completion? Even though you may be anxious, let the kids play their own game. Don't place an extra burden on them.

It is wise to leave during play and let the children play their own game. The best advice to give your child is to understand the role of the tournament director. At any time during the game, if your child feels there is a question, regardless of how simple it may seem, he should stop the clock, raise his hand and get an answer from the TD.

Another area of difficulty is determining how the child

should prepare before going to a tournament. It is glorious for a child to state he/she is going to The Nationals. However, in fairness to and respect for the parents who must share the financial and time burden of such events, I feel it imperative that the child accept some responsibility. This can vary among families. Whether it be helping with registration fees or making a commitment to study beyond the normal scope, is for the family to decide. However, I do believe that it is not enough just to show up and not have the child show due diligence to the task at hand.

Going to tournaments is one of the best ways to learn chess. However, getting into a club or camp, and having lessons has also proven to be very wise. Lessons can be found locally or on the Internet. Many community centers have lessons or clubs. If you cannot find any chess club in your area, then start one! This does not mean that you have to be proficient in chess. Some Moms have started meetings at the local library. Last year I wanted a daytime chess camp for my son. Since there wasn't one established, my son's chess coach and I teamed up and made one for ourselves. It was a wonderful success!

As parents who want to protect their children, we often fear their failure. When we realized that playing in tourna-ments was necessary, the question arose, "Is my child good enough?". How could he be expected to win if he had never played before? In other sports, there are team members to cushion a defeat. If your softball team loses, it can be mellowed by the fact that "Johnny dropped the ball" or "Sammy struck out." In chess, if you lose, you must accept all responsibility. Your win is your win, your loss is your loss. It can be a scary proposition for both parent and child.

Perhaps the most important advice we can give applies to

other arenas as well. It should be remembered that chess is a game. It is competitive in nature. However, whether you child wins or loses, it is your child's game. His success is his success alone. His failures are his failures. (Unfortunately, this is usually defined by an unexpected loss. However, the truth is that the true victor is the one who can learn from his experiences and gain strength even in the face of defeat). In all sports, upsets occur frequently. It is the excitement of the play and the battle that is the challenge.

It is most unhealthy to live vicariously from your child's accomplishments and feel defeated by his failures. Let the child determine his goals. Discuss them and see if they are reasonable. If they are low, discuss the work involved with aiming higher and the satisfaction that can come from meeting a challenge. If they are too high, discuss a more realistic dream. Perhaps more time is needed to reach the lofty expectations. Do not shatter aspirations but try to ensure that the tools are available to make them attainable.

For the Best Chess Reading: www.ChessCafe.com

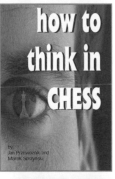